# Essential
# Austria

## by
## SALLY BRADSHAW

Sally Bradshaw has made about 20 trips to Austria in her capacity as a classical soprano. She has starred in festival productions in Innsbruck, Vienna and Eisenstadt. Often feeling inspired to write on musical trips abroad, her impressions of Austria, Poland and Malaysia have been published by *World Gastronomy*, the *Good Food Guide* and *Discovery* magazine. She has also written for *The Independent* newspaper.

**AA**

Produced by AA Publishing

Written by Sally Bradshaw
Verified by Sally Bradshaw and
Adi Kraus
Peace and Quiet section
by Paul Sterry

Revised second edition 1996
First published 1993

Edited, designed and produced by
AA Publishing.
© The Automobile Association 1993,
1996.
Maps © The Automobile Association
1993, 1996.

Distributed in the UK by AA Publishing, Norfolk House, Priestley Rd,
Basingstoke, Hampshire, RG24 9NY.

A CIP catalogue record for this book
is available from the British Library.

ISBN 0 7495 1316 0

The Automobile Association retains
the copyright in the original edition
© 1993 and in all subsequent
editions, reprints and amendments.

Published by AA Publishing, a
trading name of Automobile
Association Developments Limited,
whose registered office is Norfolk
House, Priestley Road, Basingstoke,
Hampshire, RG24 9NY.

Registered number 1878835.

Colour Reproduction by:
BTB Colour Reproduction Ltd.,
Whitchurch, Hampshire

Printed by: Printers S.R.L., Trento,
Italy

Front cover picture: *Salzkammergut*

### Maps and Plans

**Author's Acknowledgement**:
Sally Bradshaw thanks the
Austrian Tourist Board for their
help in preparing this book.

# *Contents*

---

**Country Distinguishing Signs**

On some maps, international distinguishing signs have been used to indicate the location of the countries which surround Austria.

- CH = Switzerland
- CZ = Czech Republic
- SK = Slovak Republic
- D = Germany
- FL = Liechtenstein
- H = Hungary
- I = Italy
- SLO = Slovenia

---

This book employs a simple rating system to help choose which places to visit:

 'top ten'

 ◆◆◆ do not miss
◆◆ see if you can
◆ worth seeing if you have time

# *Introduction and Background*

## INTRODUCTION

Austria radiates an almost fairytale dose of charm. Maybe it's due to a lightheadedness induced by all that mountain air, or the fact that everyone seems to be dedicated to making sure that visitors have a good time. Whatever the reason, the beauty of the scenery and the cities triggers a vitality that can only be checked by a hearty intake of Austrian cuisine – with its high quotient of meat and dumplings, noodles and cream.

Austrian images are the stuff of picture books, with a dream-like appeal that just stops short of being twee. Lush flower-strewn meadows framed by snowy peaks; cuckoo-clock chalets hung thickly with geraniums; golden-tipped

*Stunning scenery from Innsbruck*

onion-domed churches laden with cherubs and encrusted with stucco and gilt; and the grandest of palaces that evoke the power and wealth of the Habsburg Empire. The country exudes quality, whether it is in the solid workmanship of the buildings, the high standard of the public services, even the clothes people wear. It's clean without being clinical, joyous without being vacuous. In Austria, the pleasure principle rules like no other.

*Idyllic Faaker See*

## BACKGROUND

At the crossroads of Europe, a watershed between the cultures of East and West, Austria is ringed by seven other states, while the mighty Danube cuts a swathe through the north of the country. Modern Austria emerged as an independent state only after World War I, but through the centuries, its people and its lands have played a major role in central European history. Initially the country served as a frontier between the German-speaking peoples and the Slavs and Magyars to the east, but it eventually became the core of a vast empire controlled by the Habsburg family.

*Christian devotion at Corpus Christi: the liturgical year is marked by many festivals*

### Early History

First traces of man in Austria go back to palaeolithic times. In the neolithic period, salt-mining was developed at Hallein, Hallstatt and Hall (*Hall* means 'salt'). Following a Celtic period, the area began to serve as frontier outposts for the Roman Empire. Christianity began to spread into the area in about 300 AD, and as the Roman Empire crumbled, German peoples settled here. Towards the end of the 8th century Charlemagne set up a short-lived realm covering much of western Europe, of which Austria was a border province. After his death, the empire was fragmented, and the eastern, largely German-speaking part became the 'Holy Roman Empire of the German Nation'.

The first emperor, Otto the Great, defeated the Magyars at the Battle of Lechfeld in 955, and was crowned seven years later with the crown that is one of today's most valued possessions in Vienna's Imperial Treasury (Schatzkammer). In 976 the Austrian lands were committed to the Margrave Leopold of Babenberg, whose family ruled for the next 270 years, and 20 years later, the name of this area, 'Ostarrichi', was first coined. The minerals in the mountains – gold, silver and salt – began to be exploited and the province prospered; monasteries were set up and the church also accumulated wealth. The Babenberg family established their court in Vienna, an event marking the beginning of the city's significant political status.

## BACKGROUND

*Maria Theresia*

### The Habsburg Connection

In the late 13th century Austria came into the hands of the Habsburg family, whose rule was to span six centuries, and whose territorial acquisitions were enormous. The Habsburg lands began to expand far beyond German-speaking Europe, and Austria became the hub of European affairs. Although the separate German principalities enjoyed much independence, the Habsburgs still ruled. Favourable royal marriage links culminated in the early 16th century with an extraordinary accumulation of land under Habsburg Emperor Charles V. Territories under the Holy Roman Emperor included Spain and its American dominions, the Netherlands, as well as the ancestral Austrian lands.

For Austria, one of the crucial influences of this period was the advance of the Ottoman Turks. Charles V's brother Ferdinand had married into the Hungarian royal family, thus establishing claim to Bohemia, Croatia and Hungary. But the Ottomans, who had steadily expanded their rule through the Balkans, crushed Hungary in 1526. Although the Turks were beaten back from Vienna in 1529, war was now endemic on the eastern frontier. In 1556 Charles V abdicated, and his brother Ferdinand took over the eastern sector, while Philip II, Charles's son, ruled the west.

Not only did Ferdinand and his successors have to deal with the Turks threatening their eastern borders, but they also faced problems from within Germany, where there were persistent troubles arising from the challenge to Rome's authority from dissenters like Luther and Calvin. By the early 17th century these conflicts erupted in the Thirty Years' War. The Holy Roman Empire became a battleground where French and Swedish armies fought with a German-Catholic coalition led by the Habsburgs. When the conflicts had ceased, the Habsburgs had emerged as the major German-based state.

The Turks renewed their assault on Vienna in 1683, but were again repulsed. From there the Habsburgs' armies continued across the eastern frontier, overcoming the Hungarian monarchy in 1687, and on into Slav lands.

## Peace and Prosperity

In the 18th century Vienna's Habsburg court was one of the most influential in Europe. Maria Theresia (1740–80), who succeeded to the throne only after a special law was passed to allow women to rule, was one of the key Habsburgs. With able assistance, she reformed the educational, financial and legal systems, and set about promoting trade and industry.

Maria Theresia's son Joseph continued his mother's reforms, abolishing serfdom and introducing religious freedom, but he upset the population by closing monasteries.

The Habsburgs resisted the threat from Napoleon, but lost territory to him that was only returned after he was defeated.

*The last great Hapsburg Emperor, Franz-Josef*

The 18-year-old Franz-Josef ascended the throne in 1848, and was immediately beset by nationalist revolutions. Yet in spite of this unsettled beginning, he saw the transformation of Vienna from an almost medieval city to an elegant metropolis, and presided over the rich years of the city's artistic and intellectual life at the turn of the century.

The Prussians under Bismarck finally defeated Austria, and in 1867, after opting out of unification with Germany, a dual monarchy was established with separate parliaments for Austria and Hungary, but with Franz-Josef wearing both crowns. In the 19th century Austro-Hungary developed economically, but social and national tensions increased.

Austria's growth continued with the Turks' withdrawal from the Balkans. But the newly independent Slavs resented Austria's power, and matters came to an infamous climax when heir to the throne, Archduke Franz Ferdinand, was assassinated by a Serb in Sarajevo – the act that triggered World War I.

Allied to Germany, Austria's defeat in 1918 led to the dissolution of the Austro-Hungarian Empire. Out of this emerged the Republic of Austria, a relatively tiny portion of the once huge empire, bordered by newly independent states – Hungary, Czechoslovakia and the Kingdom of Yugoslavia. Parts of the old Habsburg lands were given to Italy, Poland and Romania.

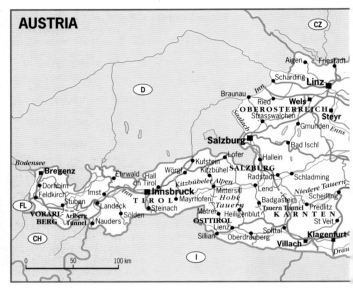

**A New Start**

The 1920s and early 1930s proved
economically difficult. Vienna was now greatly
out of proportion to the reduced size of the
country, and the break-up of old trading
patterns within the former empire was
disrupted. As elsewhere, the new democratic
procedure proved fragile. Extreme nationalists
struggled with socialists, and eventually an
authoritarian regime attempted to hold a
balance. Meanwhile, across the German
border, Hitler's Nazi party was in power,
aiming to unite all Germans. In 1938 the
Austrian chancellor proposed a plebiscite to
decide the issue, but the German army
marched in, and Austria was overrun.

After World War II Austria's pre-war frontiers
were reinstated, and the country divided into
zones which were occupied by the Allies;
Vienna was also split into four sectors. The
occupation continued until 1955, when the
Austrian State treaty was agreed. Under the
treaty, political or economic union with
Germany was forbidden, the rights of
minorities – such as Slovenes – were

*Belvedere figure, Vienna*

guaranteed, and Austria required to remain permanently neutral. However, in the years before the treaty Austria's economy had grown stronger, and recent events in eastern Europe have cast a different light on the post-war settlement.

## Austria Today

Modern Austria has been obliged to reconcile the past glories of empire with a lesser global position; in this it has been largely successful. Now a member of the United Nations and the EU, it plays host to UN agencies and numerous international conferences in Vienna one of the three main UN cities. An educated and prosperous workforce now lives in a land relatively untouched by the ravages of World War II. The old occupations of farming, forestry and mining have moved aside for industries such as steel manufacture, food processing, electrical engineering and the service sector. The sensible harnessing of natural resources like water power and timber contribute to a balanced economy operating in a clean attractive environment; and massive grants

*Alpine ceremony*

keep buildings in immaculate condition.
However the threat of pollution remains,
ironically from one of the major sources of
revenue – tourism. The new invaders, the
skiers and the summer visitors, bring with
them cars and exhaust fumes, and the demand
for new resorts and cable cars. The fragile
Alpine micro-climate is threatened, and Austria
has to decide whether more expansion will
destroy the land that feeds her. Currently, the
balance appears to be holding.

A more harmonious element is the lifestyle of
the people. The generation gap is not
especially noticeable, and family life runs on
traditional lines. More detectable is the division
between city and village life, a facet which
makes an interesting mix for the visitor.

In 1989, Austria applied for membership of the
European Community; and new opportunities
are emerging in the countries to the east. But
disorder within former Yugoslavia and the
emergence of newly independent states revive
old nationalistic and regional differences which
can still pose thorny problems.

### Art and Architecture

As ever, tensions resulting from such a
turbulent past do provide creative cultural
compensations. Until the 15th century, art was
monumental and in the service of the Christian
church. Whether it was in the construction of
huge abbeys or a mere ceiling fresco, men
focused on the other world. Little Romanesque
art remains, but what does reveals a distinct
Byzantine influence. The Gothic period,
however, has left a fine legacy. This saw the
flowering of the stone mason's and carpenter's
skills, as the Habsburgs drew on German and
Italian influences.

The Gothic ribbed vaulting and slender spires
gave way, often very slowly in the more
isolated regions, to the Renaissance style. This
was more man-centred, as the rulers wanted
art to reflect their own glory as much as that of
Heaven. However, apart from a few
magnificent examples, the Renaissance had a
short life in Austria due to the constant threat
from the Turks, which had the effect of
concentrating the energy of the populace on

war rather than on art. The benefit of this for today's visitor can be seen in the magnificent castle strongholds sprinkled throughout the east and south.

Sickened by disease and war, Europe welcomed a period of relative peace, and Austria invested her creative energies in the baroque style, which is arguably her greatest artistic epoch. Austrian baroque, with its extravagant detail, swirling lines, rich colours and textures, is a feast after famine.

Encouraged by a revitalised Catholic church, this fantasy was made real by the unleashing of extraordinary talents: in particular, those of architects Lukas von Hildebrandt, Johann Bernhard Fischer von Erlach, Jakob Prandtauer and the Italian Carlone, who created the palaces and churches for sculptors and painters such as Donner, Rottmayr, Gran, Troger, Schmidt and Maulbertsch. Below the grand masters were thousands of artisans who

*Neptune's Fountain*

## BACKGROUND

*Johann Strauss II*

shaped the stucco, gilded the domes, and carved the cherubs. Curiously it was the consistency of this effort that unified the country in a deeper way than any political vision. Austria's next significant artistic era came at the end of the 18th century, with a neoclassical movement, and a sharply contrasting 'Biedermeier' period, when an intimate and cosy style of furnishing and decoration reflected the rise of the bourgeoisie.

Vienna was the centre of great intellectual ferment during the late 19th and early 20th centuries, when the deeper unconscious impulses in the mind of man were the central concern of thinkers like Freud and playwright Schnitzler. Art reflected this with the *Jugendstil* (art nouveau) movement, led by architect Otto Wagner and the Sezession group of artists led by Gustav Klimt, whose works have idealistic, abstract and dream-like themes. This reaction against reality continued with Expressionism, which dwelt on the expression, often abstract, of emotional experiences; its master was Oskar Kokoschka, one of the great modern painters of our age.

### Music

Almost singlehandedly, Austria has accounted for the great masters of Western classical music. Many factors can be said to have contributed to this, including a long history of church music, Austria's own folk rhythms from the Alps, and Slav ones from Bohemia, elements which merged with the classical German and Italian traditions to produce a tremendous creative outpouring in the 17th and 18th centuries. Gluck and Haydn were followed by the genius of Mozart and Beethoven. Schubert, Bruckner, Liszt, Brahms, Wolf and Mahler ensured the glittering parade continued. Folk music laid the foundations of the waltz and of the Viennese operetta practised by such luminaries as Joseph Lanner, the two Strausses (father and son), von Suppé and Lehár.

This rich vein of creativity and experiment led to the contemporary sounds of 20th-century pioneers such as Schönberg, Berg and von Webern.

# *What to See*

## VIENNA (WIEN)

As capital cities go, Vienna has witnessed more party revels than most. This irrepressible frivolity greatly irritated Leopold Mozart; 'The Viennese', he complained in a letter, 'dislike and misunderstand everything serious and sensible; they care only for burlesques, harlequinades, magical tricks, farces and antics'.

Whatever the truth of this perception, enjoyment of music and dancing is part of the Viennese way of life; and it is the waltz, created here, that best provides a metaphor for the city, at once controlled and exuberant. Confident Vienna, in love with itself, has long been a pleasure ground for the rich and gifted. The past glories of empire are reflected in the splendidly preserved baroque architecture, and in the wealth of art collections which can rival any in the world.

Another side of Vienna is depicted famously in the film *The Third Man*. Here, the city's seedy streets provide a stage setting for shabby intriguers and Cold War anti-heroes.

Still flourishing, though, is the coffee house, an institution which has nurtured generations of artists and intellectuals, and which continues to delight visitors with its décor, ambience, and not least its sumptuous and distinctive fare. The '*Wiener Lebensart*' (Viennese lifestyle), a love of the good life, is much in evidence. The only myth that fails to live up to reality is that of the 'blue' Danube. Short-stay visitors to the city are likely to see only the off-shoot Danube Canal, which edges the heart of the city; those who venture a little further afield will have a chance to see the Danube proper, more likely grey than blue. Despite having 20 per cent of the national population, Vienna does not give the impression of a thrusting metropolis. Tradition is still the key to contemporary Vienna, where the past hangs lightly. Old-fashioned courtesy is still practised, the *Heuriger* and the café still form the bedrock of social life, and a visitor can make the happy transition from the creamy stucco swirls of a baroque palace to the whipped cream adorning most café confections, sometimes enjoying both at once. On free days, the Viennese continue to head for the Wienerwald or the Prater, and whatever the hour there is sure to be music in the air.

### Musicians at Home
It is possible to visit the former homes of several composers. The best ones are:

● **Figarohaus**, Domgasse 5. This is Mozart's flat (from 1784 to 1787) where he wrote *The Marriage of Figaro*.

● **Beethoven-Erinnerungsraume**, Pasqualatihaus, Mölkerbastei 8. Beethoven was a notoriously bad tenant (stories tell of how he took showers in his bedroom by emptying buckets of water over his head), and moved frequently – which accounts for the fact that he had a large number of homes in and around Vienna. In the Pasqualatihaus, Beethoven lived occasionally, between 1804 and 1815. Other houses can be found in Heiligenstadt and Grinzing, such as the 17th-century **Beethovenhaus**, Pfarrplatz 2, Grinzing, which is now a popular *Heuriger*.

● **Haydnhaus**, Haydngasse 19. Haydn's home for the last 12 years of his life, and the place where he composed *The Creation* and *The Seasons*.

● **Schubert Museum**, Nussdorferstrasse 54. The composer's birthplace has been carefully restored.

● **Johann Strauss Wohnung**, Praterstrasse 54. This is where Strauss composed the *Blue Danube* waltz.

### History
It was the Habsburgs who made Vienna. In the 13th century, the city became their capital, and it remained so until the empire collapsed in 1918. In medieval times, it gained palaces, cathedral and university, and was home to many religious orders. The city stood firm against the Turks – who made several attacks, most notably in 1683.

After that, Vienna's illustrious age really began. Mozart, Beethoven and Schubert all found inspiration here. Under Empress Maria Theresia and, more fundamentally, under Emperor Franz-Josef, the city expanded with a host of grand public buildings – including the Opera House, the Rathaus and the Parliament building. The face of Vienna was changed irrevocably as the old city walls made way for the Ringstrasse, the grand horseshoe shaped series of avenues which forms the outer boundary of the old inner city. The musical tradition continued with Brahms, Bruckner, Hugo Wolf, Mahler and Johann Strauss (father and son).

The 20th century saw a new generation of artists, designers, writers and intellectuals gather – notably Klimt, Schiele and Olbrich, Freud, Arthur Schnitzler, Hugo von Hofmannsthal and Stefan Zweig. Its reputation as one of the great centres of Western civilisation was now beyond dispute. However, the Nazi invasion of Vienna in 1938 led to the drain of much of its intelligentsia; 50,000 Viennese Jews were

*Upper Belvedere: a masterpiece*

murdered, and the city was
heavily bombed.
Since Austrian independence in
1955, the city has slowly been
restored to its former glory; it is
now the seat of many United
Nations organisations.

## WHAT TO SEE

### ◆◆
### ALBERTINA
*Augustinerstrasse 1*
The Albertina State Collection
of Graphic Art is an
extraordinarily rich collection of
drawings – including works by
Dürer, Rembrandt and Rubens
– amassed in part by Prince
Albert von Sachsen-Teschen
and Prince Eugène of Savoy.
Because of the vast size of the
collection (said to be the largest
in the world), it is displayed in
rotation (facsimiles of the rest
can be seen). In the same
building is the Austrian Film
Museum.

### ◆◆◆
### BELVEDERE
*Prinz-Eugen-Strasse 27*
This palace, designed by Lukas
von Hildebrandt and built for
Prince Eugène of Savoy, is
considered the most
impressive baroque building in
Vienna. There are two parts.
The Lower Belvedere, which
was the summer residence of
the Prince, contains medieval
and baroque Austrian art. The
Upper Belvedere is rightly
regarded as an architectural
jewel. The clever design
surmounts the problems of
repetition posed by such a
large building, by creating a
series of differing roof lines.
The extravagant stucco work
and exterior decoration,
amazingly, do not clash. This
building now houses a newly
re-opened collection of 19th-
and 20th-century Austrian
paintings, including works by
Klimt and Schiele.
Take the U-Bahn or tram to
Südbahnhof.

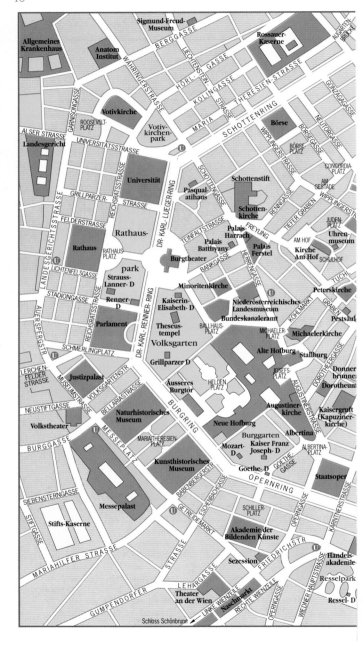

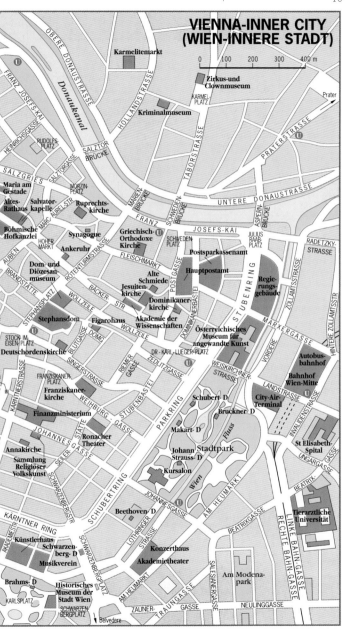

# VIENNA-INNER CITY
## (WIEN-INNERE STADT)

0   100   200   300   400 m

Zirkus-und Clownmuseum

Karmelitemarkt

Kriminalmuseum

Prater

Maria am Gestade

Altes Rathaus

Salvator-kapelle

Ruprechts-kirche

Böhmische Hofkanzlei

Synagoge

Ankeruhr

Griechisch-Orthodoxe Kirche

Postsparkassenamt

Dom- und Diözesan-museum

Alte Schmiede

Jesuiten-kirche

Hauptpostamt

Regierungs-gebäude

Dominikaner-kirche

Stephansdom

Figarohaus

Akademie der Wissenschaften

Österreichisches Museum für angewandte Kunst

Deutschordenskirche

Autobus-bahnhof

Bahnhof Wien-Mitte

Franziskaner-kirche

Schubert-D

City-Air-Terminal

Finanzministerium

Bruckner-D

Makart-D

St Elisabeth-Spital

Annakirche

Ronacher Theater

Sammlung Religiöser Volkskunst

Johann Strauss-D

Stadtpark

Kursalon

Tierärztliche Universität

Beethoven-D

Künstlerhaus

Schwarzen-berg-D

Musikverein

Konzerthaus

Akademietheater

Am Modena-park

Brahms-D

Historisches Museum der Stadt Wien

Belvedere

## ◆◆◆
## HOFBURG ✓

*Michaelerplatz*

The official residence of the Habsburg emperors for over 600 years, this enormous palace complex spans many periods – from the Gothic Hofburgkapelle, the 16th-century Schweizer Tor, the baroque Reichskanzlei (Imperial Chancellery), designed by Fischer von Erlach, through to parts of the Neue Hofburg dating from the early years of this century. A new Roman excavation can be seen by the Michaeler gate. Highlights of the complex include:

● **Burgkapelle** (Imperial chapel), Schweizerhof, home to the Vienna Boys' Choir, who sing mass here on Sunday mornings.

● **Kaiserappartements** (Imperial Apartments), a series of opulent 19th-century rooms which were home to Emperor Franz-Josef I and the Empress Elisabeth. Of particular interest are her apartments, which include her private gymnasium.

● **Schatzkammer** (Imperial Treasury), Schweizerhof, where you can see the original crown of the Holy Roman Emperor and a wonderful collection of jewellery.

● **Winterreitschule** (Winter Riding School), where the world-famous Spanish Riding School puts on public dressage displays. The beautiful white Lipizzaners perform faultlessly to music by Strauss under massive chandeliers.

Other sights in the enormous Hofburg complex include the **Hoftafel und Silberkammer Museum** (Collection of Imperial Cutlery and Silver), and museums devoted to musical instruments, arms and armour, ethnology and globes, among many others. Opening times for the different parts of the Hofburg vary. For information contact the Vienna Tourist Board at Obere Augartenstrasse 40 or Kärntnerstrasse 38. For details of how to obtain tickets for the Spanish Riding School or the Vienna Boys' Choir, see page 104.

*Fiakers outside the Hofburg Palace*

### ◆◆◆
### KUNSTHISTORISCHES MUSEUM

*Maria-Theresien-Platz*

This is one of the great fine arts museums of Europe, largely amassed by the Habsburg rulers. There are particularly large collections of works by Brueghel, Titian, Rubens and Velázquez. On the ground floor are Oriental and Egyptian sections, sculpture collections, and decorative arts. Coins and medals are on the second floor.

### ◆◆◆
### SCHÖNBRUNN ✓

*The gilded beauty of Schönbrunn's Great Gallery*

Another Fischer von Erlach masterpiece set in magnificent formal gardens and park, this rather severe ochre-coloured building was the summer palace of the Habsburgs (they spent winters at the Hofburg). Schönbrunn is most closely associated with Maria Theresia, who considered it her favourite residence. Her rococo apartments include the beautiful Hall of Mirrors, where the six-year-old Mozart gave his royal recital to the empress and her children, a magnificent Great Gallery, an intimate Chinese Room, used for private dinners, and the so-called 'Millions Room', panelled with rosewood. Throughout are many items of interest, including porcelain, paintings, and characteristic ceramic heating stoves.
In the park is the elegant Gloriette folly, a hill-top showpiece which contrasts beautifully with the strictly ordered design of the park. From here, there are particularly fine views of the city and the Wienerwald. Other attractions include a baroque theatre, sometimes used for performances, a palm-house, a butterfly house and the Wagenburg Museum – an excellent collection of imperial coaches, sleighs and sedan chairs.
Schönbrunn can be reached by underground from Karlsplatz. The apartments are accessible by guided tour, lasting 45 minutes.

### ◆
### SEZESSION

*Friedrichstrasse 12*

Built in 1898, this extraordinary gilded building near Karlsplatz encapsulates the *Jugendstil* movement (the Viennese Art Nouveau). The name refers to the union of artists who used this as their exhibition gallery – led by Gustav Klimt, whose famous Beethoven Frieze can be seen in the basement. There is a café in the building.

*Distinctively tiled Stephansdom in the heart of Vienna's pedestrian centre*

### STEPHANSDOM

St Stephen's Cathedral is Vienna's landmark: its steeple soaring above the city, its steep roof dazzling with yellow, green and black tiles and depicting the double-headed Habsburg eagle. Founded in the 13th century, the building has features from many periods, in particular the Romanesque northwest façade with its Riesentor (Giants' Door). Inside the lofty building is a fine red marble tomb of Emperor Friedrich III, and a wood pulpit 'signed' with a self-portrait by the carpenter, Anton Pilgram. Mozart was married here, and his own *Requiem* performed for him on the 200th anniversary of his death, on 5 December 1991. The South Tower can be climbed; there is lift access up the North Tower. From here you can see the huge Pummerin Bell, as well as most of the city. The catacombs can also be visited.

**Architectural Trendsetters**
Vienna has been the home of several remarkable architects, who in the early years of this century reacted against the grandiose neoclassical or Italianate-style public buildings that had been built in the last half of the 19th century – Otto Wagner (1841–1918); Josef Hoffmann (1870–1956); Josef Maria Olbrich (1867–1908); and Adolf Loos (1870–1933). The most famous example of the 'new style' is Olbrich's Sezession building (see page 21). Other fine examples include the **Post Office Savings Bank**, Georg Coch Platz 2 (Wagner); and '**Looshaus**', Michaelerplatz (Loos).
Another curious and eye-catching building is the **Hundertwasser Haus** (Löwengasse/Kegelgasse). This municipal housing complex, built in 1985, was designed by the painter Friedensreich Hundertwasser to be built only of natural materials.

## EXCURSIONS FROM VIENNA

◆◆

### THE PRATER AND THE DANUBE

The Prater is Vienna's main amusement park, its landmark the giant Riesenrad (Ferris Wheel) was immortalised in Orson Welles' *The Third Man*. Other rides include rollercoasters, dodgems, and a miniature railway; and there is plenty of live entertainment. The area beside the funfair is partly wooded, and there are ponds and meadows. It was here that Emperor Franz Josef I used to ride on horseback every morning, and Empress Elisabeth would be driven to take the morning air. By the Danube are cycle tracks, bathing beaches and cafés. Boats can be hired, and summer river excursions are offered by the DDSG (Danube Steamship Company).

◆◆◆

### WIENERWALD

*20 miles (32km) west of Vienna*
The most popular day trip is into the Vienna Woods, former hunting grounds of royals and aristocrats. Here there are waymarked paths, and the Lainzer Tiergarten Nature Protection Area. It is also vineyard country, and the wine villages are full of *Heurigen*, places where you can drink the new wine (often to the accompaniment of music). Some of the villages are almost suburbs of Vienna, and not particularly special. **Grinzing** is

*See Vienna from the Prater Wheel*

one of the best known, and consequently generally full of tourists; **Heiligenstadt**, **Nussdorf** and **Neustift am Walde** are preferred by locals. See also **The East** (page 27) for: Dürnstein, Eisenstadt, Heiligenkreuz, Klosterneuburg, Krems, Mayerling and Melk.

## PRACTICAL VIENNA

### Shopping

The main shopping areas are: Kärntnerstrasse and Graben (pedestrianised), and Mariahilfer Strasse. **Lobmeyr**, at Kärntnerstrasse 12, sells special gifts, particularly glassware; **Augarten**, Stock-im-Eisen Platz 3–4, is famous for its hand-painted porcelain. Traditional Austrian 'Loden' coats are available from **Lanz**, Kärntnerstrasse, **Lodenplankl**, Michaelerplatz, and **Tostmann** in Schottengasse. Typical embroidery can be bought in **Smejkal** in Opernpassage; and handicrafts at **Österreichische Werkstätten**, Kärntnerstrasse 6. The **Naschmarkt**, on Linke Wienzeile (open daily except Saturday afternoon and Sunday), sells food; at the southern end is the **Flohmarkt** (Flea Market) – take the U4 to Kettenbrückengasse.

# VIENNA

---

### Viennese coffee
Viennese coffee comes in a large variety of styles: *Brauner* (dark white), *Melange* (lighter white), *Verlängerter* (frothy white), *Einspänner* (tall glass, black with whipped cream), *Mokka* (small, strong and black), *Türkischer* (small, thick and sweet), *mit Schlag* (with whipped cream), *mit Doppelschlag* (with two scoops of double whipped cream)…

---

## Food and Drink

### The Coffee House
A popular tale about the origin of coffee in Vienna maintains that in the 17th century a few beans left behind by the departing Turkish invaders started a trend for coffee drinking which continues to this day. Whatever the truth of this, Viennese coffee houses are an institution. Here, people sit for hours, reading newspapers, holding meetings, and writing letters. Some are famous for their architecture, as well as their coffee.

A short selection might include: the **Café Central** in the Palais Ferstel, Herrengasse/Strauchgasse (like a Venetian palace); **Demel**, Kohlmarkt 14 (favoured by Kaiser Franz-Josef, in rich baroque style with mirrors and gilt); **Café Hawelka**, Dorotheergasse 6, off Graben (old haunt of bohemians and intellectuals – known for its *Buchteln*, choux filled with plum jam); **Café Sperl**, Karolinengasse 13 (mahogany, brass and billiards, with the atmosphere of a gentlemen's club); **Café Sacher**, Philharmonikerstrasse 4 (for the most famous chocolate cake of them all).

### The Beisl
The traditional Viennese tavern is a good place to go to for simple and inexpensive food. There are scores of *Beisl*; recommended ones include **Zum Alten Fassl**, Ziegelhofengasse 37 (the regular haunt of the Wiener Philharmoniker Orchestra); **Purstner**, Riemergasse 10 (very large helpings of *Hausmannskost*); and **Peter's Beisl**, Arnethgasse 98 (known for good Sunday lunches and game).

### Vegetarian and Snack Restaurants
**Legume**, Währingerstrasse 57, and **Dinkel-Löwe**, in the Hundertwasser House, Löwengasse 41–3, serve vegetarian dishes. **Trzesniewski**, Dorotheergasse 1 or Mariahilfer Strasse 28–30, is excellent for a quick snack, and offers a huge range of open sandwiches, draught beer and *Apfelmost* (cider).

### Bars and *Heurigen*
Wine and beer drinkers are amply catered for, both in cafés and in bars. Some bars have a special feature – such as **Santo Spirito**, Kimpfgasse 7 (classical music); **Roter Engel,** Rabensteig 5/16 (live music); **Jazzland**, Franz-Josefs-Kai 29 (live jazz). Information about current 'popular hangouts' is given in the brochure *Youth Scene*, available from the tourist office.

The area around the Ruprechtskirche (between Hohe Markt and the Donau Kanal) is known as the 'Bermuda Triangle', so called because within it are so many wine bars that it is possible to disappear. The best places in which to sample wine, or at least young wine, are the *Heurigen*, wine-taverns where growers sell the produce from their vineyards. (See **Wienerwald**).

**Entertainment**
For information about opera, theatre, dance, concerts, festivals, and performances of the Spanische Reitschule (Spanish Riding School) and Wiener Sängerknaben (Vienna Boys' Choir), including how to obtain tickets, see **Culture, Entertainment and Nightlife** on pages 101 to 105.

*Burgtheater: classic performances*

## VIENNA

### Accommodation

Vienna has a very wide variety of hotels in all categories, including some very grand hotels set in memorable buildings. One of the finest, in part of a baroque palace, is **Im Palais Schwarzenberg,** Schwarzenbergplatz 9 (tel: 1-7984515), with a large park and swimming pool – yet only 10 minutes' walk from the Ring. Another famous luxury hotel is the turn-of-the-century **Bristol**, Kärntner Ring 1 (tel: 1-515160), all in appropriate marble-and-velvet style. Near by, opposite the Opera House, the **Sacher**, Philharmonikerstrasse 2 (tel: 1-51456) frequented by royalty and known for its *Sachertorte* (chocolate cake), is similarly styled, and offers a variety of bars, restaurants and, of course, cafés.

Less expensive, but still very atmospheric, is the four-star **König von Ungarn,** Schulerstrasse 10 (tel: 1-515840), near Stephansdom, built around a fine old courtyard (now glass-domed). The simpler three-star **Kärntnerhof**, Grashofgasse 4 (tel: 1-5121923) is quietly situated and unpretentious, with spacious bedrooms.

Vienna has plenty of *pensionen* (bed-and-breakfast), also star-rated. In the four-star category, the **Pension Pertschy**, Habsburgergasse 5 (tel: 1-53449) is well placed near the Graben, and has modern furnishings. Similarly well situated near the Opera House, the three-star **Pension Suzanne**, Walfischgasse 4 (tel: 1-5132507) is relaxed and old-fashioned.

### Tourist Office

Vienna Tourist Board, Obere Augartenstrasse 40, A-1025 Vienna (tel: 1-211140). The main information office is at Kärntnerstrasse 38 (tel: 1-5138892).

*The home of the famous Sachertorte*

# THE EAST

Eastern Austria is a very mixed bag of delights, taking in the architectural and natural splendours of the Danube valley, the orchards and vineyards of the north, and in the south, Burgenland with its castles and shallow lake, the Neusiedler See. Beauty and history go hand-in-hand almost undisturbed, and unlike many other areas of Europe which have a capital city in their midst, eastern Austria is not overshadowed by Vienna, but is interesting in its own right. For the purposes of this book, the east here means most of the province of Niederösterreich (Lower Austria), the outer Vienna basin and the province of Burgenland.

It is the River Danube which dominates – the vital artery that has constantly brought new peoples and cultures into the region through the centuries. In terms of beauty the Wachau Valley stretch reigns supreme, with turreted castles and domed abbeys impossibly poised on crags high above the waters. Vineyards flourish here too, as do soft fruit orchards and vegetables. The legacy of the area's history is reflected in the decorative small towns, like Dürnstein, where churches, monasteries, museums and even ordinary homes brim with past glories of every age, from the Romanesque to the 19th century – with the baroque era especially well represented. Northeast of Vienna lies the rolling Weinviertel (wine area) where along with vineyards

*Klosterneuberg's renowned abbey*

and arable farming there is oil exploration in the east. Further west the scenery changes as the land rises to become the less populous wooded Waldviertel (forest area). Burgenland, which extends south from the Czech and Slovak borders to the Slovenian/Hungarian frontiers, was a political football for centuries. Celts, Romans, Slavs and Turks all pitched in at varying stages, and most recently the Germans and the Soviet armies had a bitter battle for control during World War II. As a consequence, Burgenland's ancient buildings have been razed and restored continually, so evidence of early history has been virtually wiped out. However, a plethora of castles and strongholds remain, as the name of the province (Burgenland means 'land of castles') testifies. The cultural legacy inevitably is varied. Here are villages with definite

# THE EAST

Slav overtones. You may see gaily painted wagons, low, white Hungarian-style cottages, and be served meat stews with more than a dash of paprika. Burgenland is unique in other ways too. From the eastern edge of the strange reed-fringed Neusiedler See, the dusty flat *puszta* (steppe) unravels into the distance. Little lake-side villages are dotted along the shore, full of flowers. Some storks come here to nest, usually in the middle of town. In summer Burgenland is sunny and dry, the wine flows freely, and music can always be heard in the taverns or cafés – whether it be the strains of a classical trio or a gypsy guitar.

*Pestsäule (plague monument), Baden bei Wien*

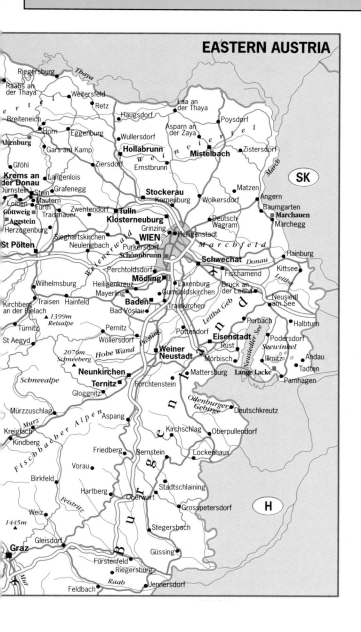

# EASTERN AUSTRIA

## THE EAST

## WHAT TO SEE

### BADEN BEI WIEN
*Niederösterreich*
For centuries the healing waters
of Austria's principal spa town
have soothed emperors,
composers and socialites as
well as the sick. Tucked in the
southeastern edge of the
Wienerwald (Vienna Woods)
and 18 miles (29km) from
Vienna, Baden lies on the banks
of the River Schwechat. The
Romans called it *Aquae* and
developed its thermal springs;
but the town reached
prominence in the 18th and
19th centuries when the
Viennese flocked to take its
sulphurous water and mud
cures. Mozart and his wife
visited; Beethoven stayed
regularly. It became a summer
favourite with the Habsburg
court, especially Emperor
Franz I. Evidence of this
patronage is demonstrated in
the town's Biedermeier style.
Baden is still a popular spa.
Fifteen springs pour out around
7 million litres of water warmed
to body temperature – ideal for
those suffering from
rheumatism, arthritis or stress.
Ten health centres, catering for
15,000 people, offer a huge
variety of hydrotherapies.
There are parks, treatment
centres, and swimming pools of
every kind, plus a sandy beach
by the Schwechat River in
Helenenstrasse.
In the tranquil **Kurpark** (cure
park) to the north of the centre
is an ornate 19th-century
casino, and an open-air theatre
(Arena) which stages an
operetta season from June to
September. To the north of the
park are superb walks with
views overlooking the resort.
Naturally, Baden also has a full
range of sporting activities,
including tandem parachuting
and trotting races.
In the town centre, there are
several things of interest. In the
Hauptplatz stands an 18th-
century **Pestsäule** (Plague
Tower), the 19th-century
**Rathaus** and the **Kaiserhaus**,
Emperor Franz I's summer
residence. The baroque
imperial **Frauenkirche** (Church
of Our Lady) has a neoclassical
interior. The **Beethovenhaus**, a
small museum at Rathausgasse
10, is where the composer lived
and composed part of the Ninth
Symphony.
The *Heurigen* (see box on
**Wine**, page 35) resemble those
of Vienna, and display a pole
outside decked with pine twigs.
The addresses of those
currently open are posted
around town.

### Accommodation and Restaurants
**Grand Hotel Sauerhof**,
Weilburgstrasse 16, A-2500
(tel: 2252-412510), a former
palace in a magnificent setting,
and the elegant **Hotel Schloss
Weikersdorf**, Schlossgasse
9–11 (tel: 2252-48301) are two
expensive options. Cheaper
are the **Strandbad Hotel
Pension Eden**, Schlossgasse 42
(tel: 2252-433920) and the
three-star **Haus Rainer Ring**,
Erherzog-Rainer-Ring 17 (tel:
2252-48291).
There is a good café at the **Hotel
Sacher**, at Helenenstrasse 55.

## Tourist Office
Kurdirektion Baden, Hauptplatz 2, A-2500 Baden bei Wien (tel: 2252-86800).

## Excursions
About 9 miles (15km) northeast of Baden, the small market town of **Laxenburg** has a lovely park, 18th-century mansions, and a former imperial palace. The **Neues Schloss** (1752) was Empress Maria Theresia's summer residence, and it is now the headquarters of an international organisation. Concerts and plays are performed in the theatre. The medieval **Altes Schloss** was rebuilt after 1683; it now contains the Austrian film archives, and films are shown in summer. Near by, on a lake island, is the gothic Franzenburg, which houses Habsburg memorabilia, paintings and furniture. Equestrian events are held in the park.

Nine miles (15km) northwest of

*Ludwig van Beethoven, moody genius of Vienna*

Baden is **Mayerling**, a Carmelite convent which marks the place where a tragic love story reached its finale. In 1888 the dissolute Archduke Rudolf, son and heir of Emperor Franz-Josef, fell in love with teenage Maria Vetsera. His father bitterly opposed the liaison, and overcome by his political problems Rudolf resolved on a double suicide. In January 1889 he went to the imperial hunting lodge at Mayerling with Maria. She died first, then Rudolf wrote a suicide note and shot himself. The convent was erected by the distraught emperor, and is of little interest in its own right; visitors are able to enter a small chapel.

The Cistercian abbey of **Heiligenkreuz**, 3 miles (5km) from Mayerling, is surrounded by woods, and has an impressive and typically severe Romanesque church.

## ◆◆◆
### DÜRNSTEIN ✓

*Niederösterreich*

Perched on a ridge beside a sweeping arc of the Danube in the Wachau region (see separate entry), Dürnstein is undeniably romantic. The village, despite being rather commercialised, is very picturesque; and terraced vineyards and castle ruins embrace its rim. Dürnstein's famous monastery, founded by Augustinians, is notable for its ornate cloister and stucco work; the baroque tower is a landmark in the region.

A steep 30-minute climb above

*Romantic ruins above Dürnstein*

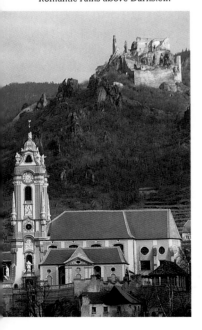

the village takes you to the ruins of a 12th-century castle where Richard the Lionheart was held prisoner, and from which he was released only after a huge ransom had been paid. Local legends say the minstrel Blondel discovered his master here.

### Accommodation

Five-star **Hotel Schloss Dürnstein**, A-3601 (tel: 2711-212) is beautifully set in a 17th-century mansion overlooking the Danube. Close to the river, the four-star **Hotel Richard Löwenherz**, (tel: 2711-222), is situated in an old convent building. More modest establishments include the three-star **Gasthof Sänger Blondel**, (tel: 2711-253), in a pretty building with a garden.

## ◆◆◆
### EISENSTADT

*Burgenland*

The capital of Burgenland is renowned as a centre for wine. It is a very small and pleasant old city, favoured by a mild climate which allows soft fruits and almonds, as well as vines, to grow.

In 1622 Emperor Ferdinand gave the town to the Esterházy family, a Hungarian clan who could trace their ancestry to Attila the Hun. Eisenstadt blossomed culturally under the Esterházy's aristocratic rule and was made a royal free city. It remained Hungarian until the early 1920s when it elected to be part of Austria after the break-up of the Austro-Hungarian Empire.

The town is also famous as the home of Joseph Haydn; the composer lived here for 30 years. In Freistadt, the old city centre, is the **Haydn Museum** (in Haydngasse). The composer maintained that 'Eisenstadt is where I wish to live and die'. The house also contains a memorial to the composer Franz Liszt.

**Schloss Esterházy** dominates the town centre. This large ochre baroque palace was built for the Esterházy family in the late 17th century by the Italian Carlo Carlone. Haydn conducted his works in the ornately decorated Haydn Saal and praised its acoustics. Concerts, often in period costume, are performed on Tuesdays and Thursdays at 11.00hrs. Guided tours are available.

The **Franziskanerkirche** (Franciscan church) contains an antique organ which Haydn considered his favourite organ ('meine Lieblingsorgel'). Indeed, it has to this day a woody mellow sound. Haydn's tomb is in the baroque **Bergkirche**, in the west of the town; his wish to be laid to rest in Eisenstadt was finally granted years after his death in Vienna.

There are a couple of museums of note in Eisenstadt. In Unterbergstrasse is the **Österreichisches Jüdisches Museum** (Austrian Jewish Museum), housed in the old barred ghetto which existed from 1675 to 1938. The history of all Austrian Jews is charted here, and near by there is a reconstructed Jewish cemetery. To the east, at Museumgasse 5, is the **Burgenländisches Landesmuseum** (Provincial Museum), exploring folk art and natural history.

---

**Burgenland Castles**

**Bernstein** (*about 45 miles (71km) southwest of Eisenstadt*) A 12th-century fortress, rebuilt in the 17th. It has an impressive knights' hall. Part is now a hotel.

**Forchtenstein** (*about 3 miles (5km) southwest of Mattersburg*) This fortress on a high rock served as a bulwark against the Turks; it now houses paintings, arms, armour and carriages.

**Güssing** (*about 43 miles (52km) south of Bernstein*) On a solitary crag, the Batthyány Schloss displays paintings and arms, and contains a notable organ.

**Halbturn** (*on the east side of the Neusiedler See*) This fine baroque building, once an imperial hunting lodge, has ceiling paintings by Maulbertsch and a fine park.

**Stadschlaining** (*7 miles (11km) south of Bernstein*) This fine 13th-century castle with huge walls has been much altered; it now has a hotel and a folk museum.

---

**Entertainment**

Haydn is top of the list in this city. There is now an international Haydn Festival in September. For information contact the **Haydnfestspiele**, Schloss Esterházy, A-7000, Eisenstadt (tel: 2682-61866). It is also possible to hear jazz and folk in cafés in the town and in the new **Kulturzentrum Cadillac** in Mattersburgstrasse.

*Schloss Esterházy in Eisenstadt*

## Accommodation

There is a good choice, from friendly, traditional and unpretentious hotels to modern purpose-built ones. The **Gasthof zum Haydnhaus**, Haydngasse 24 (tel: 2682-64636) has a pleasant atmosphere and is very reasonably priced. **Hotel Burgenland**, Schubertplatz 1 (tel: 2682-696) is a large, modern building with an indoor swimming pool. It offers special rates for families.
Bed and breakfast places are available, too. **Toth Ewald**, Vicedom 5 (tel: 2682-64222) is very cheap.

## Restaurants

The **Schlosstaverne** is excellent value, and has a view of the Schloss Esterházy too.
**Haydnbräu**, Pfarrgasse 22, is an old brewery, providing good local fare, which has many Hungarian touches. As in

Hungary, goose washed down with new wine is eaten on 11 November (the day of St Martin, who was the patron saint of publicans and innkeepers).

### Tourist Office

Fremdenverkehrsamt der Freistadt Eisenstadt, Hauptstrasse 35, A-7000 Eisenstadt (tel: 2682-67390).

◆
### HORN

*Niederösterreich, north of Krems*
In the eastern Waldviertel (see separate entry), this small town has some fine Renaissance and baroque houses, and three notable churches. The **Pfarrkirche Hl Stephan** (St Stephen's Parish Church) has a baroque chapel; near by are the 17th-century **Piaristenkirche** and the late 16th-century **Hl George**. In Wienerstrasse 4, the **Hobarth Museum** has prehistoric and folk art exhibits; in the same building, the **Mader Museum** has an agricultural collection.

### Excursions

**Eggenburg**, 8 miles (13km) east of Horn, is a picturesque medieval town with a pillory and buildings displaying sgraffito decoration. There's also the **Krahuletz Museum**, which features a prehistoric ,exhibition.
Near the Czech border west of Horn, the local museum in the town of **Gmünd** testifies to the long tradition of glass production and stone carving in this region. Several of the town's houses have sgraffito decoration.

## Wine

Good wine flows freely in eastern Austria. Indeed, to sit outside a tavern with a brimming glass of chilled white wine amid the flowers and sun of Burgenland, or on a terrace of a fairytale castle high above the Danube, are simple holiday pleasures second to none.

Of Austria's 30,000 wine growers, many are small-scale, yet between them they produce 79 million gallons (3.6 million hectolitres) a year – 83 per cent of that white wine. Many monasteries – most notably Klosterneuburg and Heiligenkreuz – have their own label, and sometimes have museums of viticulture.

Not to be missed are the *Heurigen*, a feature of life unique to Vienna and the east. The name *Heurigen* refers both to the new season's wine and the taverns which sell it. The term means 'this year's' and only the taverns selling new wine grown in their own vineyards can adopt this title. To advertise, *Heurigen* place a pine branch, often decked with red and white ribbons, outside the door; sometimes the name '*Buschenschank*' is put up. Generally one sits outdoors at wooden tables, fortified both by the tart, fruity wine and clean air, and accompanied by accordion music.

Niederösterreich (Lower Austria) is the biggest wine producer; The Wachau region, around Dürnstein, produces some of Austria's best white wines – fruity and spicy, most from the Grüner Veltliner grape. Krems is one of the main centres of production, with an annual wine fair in May, a huge co-operative and a viticultural museum.

The huge Weinviertel, north of Vienna, produces mainly light white wines. In the extreme northwest of the region, Retz is a leading centre.

Just south of Vienna, the Thermenregion is known mainly for the pretty resort of Gumpoldskirchen, which produces some very fine white wines. Even nearer to Vienna, the suburb of Grinzing has become famous for its delicious *Heurigen* wines.

Burgenland is another major area of wine production, notable for its sweet wines; the most famous centre here is Rust.

In the extreme south of the country, Styria produces greatly improved white wines; Kloch is the main wine town of the region.

*Sun-drenched vineyards at Nussberg*

## KLOSTERNEUBERG
*Niederösterreich*

At the edge of the Wienerwald
(Vienna Woods) and just over
7 miles (12km) north of Vienna,
this village's Augustinian abbey
(Stift Klosterneuberg) is justly
renowned. The abbey buildings
overlook the Danube and
developed as the result of a gift
by the 12th-century Margrave
Leopold III, who became a
saint. The abbey represents a
range of styles ranging from
Romanesque to gothic.
Especially beautiful are the
enamelled Verdun altarpiece
(1181) found in the
Leopoldskapelle (chapel), 15th-
century stained glass windows,
frescos and marble hall.
The abbey owns some of the
largest vineyard sites in Austria,
and much viticultural research
goes on here. In Nussdorf
nearby, there are some
excellent opportunities for wine
tasting.

## KREMS AN DER DONAU
*Niederösterreich*

Situated along the northern
bank of the Danube and at the
mouth of the Krems valley,
surrounded by the Wachau
area of vineyards, Krems is one
centre of the Austrian wine
trade. It is an excellent starting
point for touring: the areas of
the Wachau, the
Nibelungengau and the
Waldviertel (see separate
entries) are all accessible.
Krems itself is a beautiful
medieval and Renaissance
town, which has grown to join
the village of Stein (see

separate entry) which lies to the
west. The town's engineering
and chemical industries do not
spoil the effect for visitors, who
will enjoy strolling its old
picturesque streets, where
traffic is banned, with perhaps a
stop at one of the many cafés or
shops.

In the **Landstrasse**, the main
street in the Old Town, several
Gothic burgers' houses still
stand, as well as the medieval
**Steiner Tor** (Stein Gate) with its
baroque tower – one of the
town's key landmarks. The
street has several 16th- and
17th-century houses flanked by
charming courtyards, such as
the Alte Post at no 32. The
**Rathaus** (1453) has a superb
oriel window.

The **Pfarrkirche Hl Veit** (Parish
Church) has undergone several
facelifts, Gothic then baroque,
after its Romanesque origins. Its
ceiling paintings are by Martin
Johann Schmidt (1718–1801), a
prolific baroque artist who lived
in Krems – hence his nickname
'Kremser'. More examples of
his altar work are in the Gothic
**Piaristenkirche** (Church of the
Order of Piarists) near by. At
Hoher Markt 5, the
**Sgraffitohaus** has superbly
decorated walls. Und, the
district between Krems and
Stein, has the restored **Kloster
Und** (Und Monastery), now
home to a wine college.

### Accommodation

A good three-star hotel is
**Donauhotel Krems**, Edmund
Hofbauerstrasse 19 (tel: 2732-
87565); **Unter den Linden**,
Schillerstrasse 5 (tel: 2732-
82115) is a three-star inn.

*The Benedictine Abbey at Melk, a landmark for miles around*

### ◆◆◆ MELK ✓

*Niederösterreich*

The green dome and yellow-and-white towers of Stift Melk (Melk Abbey) rising from the distance form one of the matchless sights of Europe. Set on a promontory above the south bank of the Danube, it is as if Melk sets out to overwhelm or subdue all within its orbit. Built by Jakob Prandtauer and Joseph Munggenast, the interior does not disappoint either. As one of the finest examples of baroque anywhere, the abbey captivates 100,000 visitors a year. It was also the setting for the best-selling medieval mystery story *The Name of the Rose*, by Umberto Eco. Highlights of an abbey tour, which lasts about an hour, include:

● **Stiftskirche** (Abbey Church), with its magnificent dome, multitude of windows, frescos, paintings, carved pulpit and organ, all set against a gold-embellished interior. The works of Austrian baroque masters Paul Troger and Michael Rottmayr are richly represented.

● **Bibliothek** (Library), containing almost 100,000 books and 2,000 manuscripts from the 9th to 15th centuries. The scientific writings of the early English Christian, the Venerable Bede, are kept here.

● **Marmorsaal** (Marble Hall), which has glorious russet marble and stucco columns, and paintings extolling wisdom and moderation.

● **Kaisergang** (Emperors' Gallery) and **Kaiserzimmer** (Imperial Room), reached via an explosion of carved cherubs on the **Kaiserstiege** (Imperial Staircase). The gallery has paintings of Austria's rulers, and the rooms document the abbey's history.

### Accommodation

The three-star hotel **Goldener Ochs**, (tel: 2752-2367) and **Gasthof Zur Post** (tel: 2752-2345) are both in Linzerstrasse.

# THE EAST

*The pleasures of Neusiedler See*

## NEUSIEDLER SEE
*Burgenland*

A short tram ride or drive east of Eisenstadt is the Neusiedler See, a steppe lake with no surface drainage – unique in Europe. It measures 22 miles by 3 to 9 miles wide (35km by 5–15km), but is very shallow and has been known to dry up. Nonetheless it is the nearest thing the Viennese have to the seaside and is very popular. Indeed, the flat steppe stretching from the eastern shore, the reeds which encircle it, and the superb birds and wildlife all make it a strange, almost compelling place (see **Peace and Quiet**, page 87). Fears over rising pollution levels have prompted a plan to turn the area into a cross-border national park including both Hungary and Austria. The surrounding villages are delightful – full of flowers and lively cafés that avoid being unpleasantly commercial – and the vineyards serve them well.

The main towns and villages are Rust, Mörbisch, Podersdorf, and Neusiedl-am-See.
**Rust**, on the western shore, is probably the most popular town, and produces notable wines. It has Renaissance and baroque houses which have an added attraction when storks come annually to nest. The Gothic **Fischerkirche** (Fishermen's Church) has lovely frescos. The *Heurigen* are great fun.
To the south is **Mörbisch**, near the Hungarian border, again a delight – particularly between July and August when the Mörbischer Seefestspiele (Lake Operetta Festival) is held. Spectators should remember their insect-repellant. The dessert wine from local vineyards is recommended.
**Podersdorf** in the east boasts the best beach, good bathing, a pleasant little local museum and some jolly cafés. The area around here is very good for rambling, with many marked paths.

The village of **Neusiedl-am-See** is on a direct route from Vienna and the nearby lake has good facilities for watersports.

### Tourist Office
Landesfremdenverkehrsamt für das Burgenland (Regional Tourist Office), Schloss Esterházy, A-7000 Eisenstadt (tel: 2682-3384).

◆
### NIBELUNGENGAU
*Niederösterreich*
Along this part of the Danube the scenery subtly changes from the terraced vineyards of the east to an Alpine aspect, and the climate, too, is chillier. The valley's mythic name refers to the Nibelungen who, legend has it, were a tribe of dwarves robbed of gold. Wagner drew on this tale for his opera *Der Ring des Nibelungen*. However the name also stuck to a group of 5th-century warriors whose exploits were immortalised in a 12th-century song well known throughout central Europe. Part of the story – a complicated one of passion, death and revenge – took place in this valley, hence its name.
To the east of a huge curve in the river known as the Böse Beuge (Wicked Bend), on a hill, stands the highly decorative **Maria Taferl**, a pilgrims' church (1661–1711) where an image of the Virgin was reportedly once seen. The towers were built by Melk's grand master Prandtauer. Some of the best views of the Danube and mountains beyond can be seen from here.
On the north bank of the river is **Schloss Artstetten**; Archduke

Franz Ferdinand, whose murder in Sarajevo triggered World War I, is buried here.
**Pöchlarn**, on the south bank of the Danube, is a little town full of traditional late Gothic and baroque architecture. The church has altarpieces by Kremser Schmidt. Oskar Kokoschka, the expressionist artist (1886–1980), was born here, and there is a research centre and small museum with exhibitions devoted to his work. It's worth making an excursion from the south bank to **Schallaburg**, 5 miles (8km) southeast of Melk. This is a fine Renaissance palace which is now used as an international exhibition centre. Its arcaded courtyard, with terracotta work, is remarkable.

◆◆
### RIEGERSBURG
*Styria*
This mighty castle east of Graz stood firm against Turkish invaders and has never been stormed successfully. It passed in the 19th century to the Princes of Liechtenstein, and during World War II it was bitterly fought over by Germans and Russians. Riegersburg has a Gothic chapel, a well-decorated Knights' hall and state rooms, and a museum of witchcraft and magic. Most of the existing edifice was built in 1650 by Elisabeth von Galler – also known as 'wicked Liesel' because of her ruthlessness. The great attraction of Riegersburg, however, is the spectacular view over miles of Styrian countryside.

### STEIN
*Niederösterreich*

This gem of a village, closely linked to Krems, is reached by walking through the district of Und. An apricot liqueur brandy, Bailoni, is distilled here, and indeed many of the houses are decorated with fruit paintings. Despite its Renaissance squares, walled boundary and river views, Stein is not inundated with tourists, nor is there any real exploitation of its charms. Just off the pedestrianised centre, the former **Minoritenkirche** (Minorite Church of St Ulrich) now hosts art exhibitions. The Gothic **Pfarrkirche Hl Nikolaus** (St Nicholas Parish Church) has frescos by Kremser Schmidt, who lived in an ornate house opposite the Linzer Tor (Linz Gate). Every house in **Steiner Landstrasse** is a visual treat – especially no. 76 (Grosser Passauerhof), the home of the Bishop of Passau, which is unmistakable, with its profusion of ornate towers and crenellations.

### Accommodation and Restaurants

The four-star **Hotel am Forthof** (tel: 2732-83345) serves good-value local food and has a fine view of the Danube.

### Excursion

A short drive, 4 miles (6km), south is the Benedictine abbey of **Stift Göttweig**, designed (1719) by Lukas von Hildebrandt; it's a mighty presence on top of a hill and visible from afar. Napoleon stayed here, and its lavish baroque interior and 15th-century stained-glass windows have long been considered one of the highlights on a visitor's itinerary. The abbey's own wines are highly regarded, as are its restaurant and wonderful views.

### TULLN
*Niederösterreich*

On the south bank of the Danube, northeast of Vienna, this Roman town was mentioned in tales of the Nibelungen. The 20th-century artist Egon Schiele was born here; there is a museum devoted to him at Donaulände 72.

Tulln's Romanesque and Gothic **Pfarrkirche** (Parish Church) has a superbly carved west door, and the neighbouring charnel house (1260) is likewise one of the best of its kind.

To the west, **Zwentendorf** has an obsolete nuclear power station which was built but never came into operation, as the Austrian people rejected it after a referendum in the late 1970s.

### WACHAU
*Niederösterreich*

The 18-mile (30-km) run between Melk and Krems (see separate entries) is the loveliest part of the Danube. A description of the rocky valley between forested uplands can do little justice to a scene which was, and is, the stuff of fairytales. The silhouette of castles, walled towns, crumbling towers and terraced vineyards resembles a collar of fine lace strung out along the blue ribbon of the river.

Autumn and spring are the least crowded times to appreciate this spectacle, but midsummer's night (21 June) has a magic without equal, as countless bonfires are lit along the water's edge and parties go on beyond dawn.

A boat trip is probably the most romantic way to visit, but a slow train west from Krems to St Valentin near Linz is a good second option.

One of the Wachau villages has achieved renown as the place where one of the earliest examples of Western art, a squat fertility goddess from the early Stone Age, was found. The Willendorf Venus is now in Vienna's Naturhistorisches Museum (Natural History Museum).

These are a few of the highlights of a journey along the Wachau valley:

● **Burg Aggstein** was the home of the Kuenringer family, a posse of highwaymen who attacked passing trade convoys. These did not stand much chance of escape as the castle stood 1,000 feet (300m) on a crag above the river. Now the massive building is in ruins, but there is still plenty to see of

*The unassailable Burg Aggstein*

the towers, kitchen, halls and walls. The views are breathtaking.

● **Dürnstein** (see separate entry).

● **Mautern**, on the south bank, is a pretty town with a toll bridge. It has an early Gothic church and a museum with Roman remains. There are some attractive walks through the vineyards.

● **Schönbühel**, also on the south bank and the gateway to the Wachau, is an attractive market town with a lovely castle (which is in private hands).

● **Spitz an der Donau**, is also a market town whose neighbouring hill, the Tausendeimerberg (Hill of a Thousand Buckets), gives an indication of its chief product. Vineyards and orchards surround it, and the ruins of the Schloss Hinterhaus stand guard above. The parish church is Gothic, and the balconies and arcades of the Renaissance and baroque houses are charming.

● **Weissenkirchen** is yet another picture-book village with a Gothic parish church and a local history museum in a 16th-century farm. A cycle ride is a good way to take in the lovely countryside.

*Medieval book illustration, Zwettl*

## Castles and Monasteries of the Waldviertel

**Altenburg** (*about 26 miles (41km) north of Krems*) This glorious Benedictine abbey with its ornately carved tower was founded in 1144, rebuilt in the 17th century and restored after Russian occupation in World War II. The Stiftsgebäude (abbey buildings) include a huge library embellished with statues and sculptures. Beneath is a strange crypt decorated with grotesque dance of death figures. A massive Kaiserstiege (Imperial Staircase) with Troger frescos leads to the lavish Marmortrakt (apartments), awash with gold plate, statues and paintings. Images of dwarves seem particularly popular. The Stiftskirche (Abbey Church) reveals some of Paul Troger's finest ceiling work, set off by pastel columns and gilt work. Guided tours are available.
**Heidenreichstein** (*about 12½ miles (20km) north of Gmünd*) This is one of the finest moated castles in Lower Austria; the ramparts and drawbridges date from the 13th century.
**Rosenau** (*5½ miles (9km) west of Zwettl*) Schloss Rosenau, renovated 20 years ago, contains Europe's only museum of freemasonry. There are allegorical frescos by Daniel Gran and Paul Troger, a reconstruction of lodge rooms and an 18th-century temple. Although originally 16th century, the castle was restored in rococo style. A hotel and restaurant are attached.
**Stift Zwettl** (*2 miles (3km) northeast of Zwettl*) Set above the agreeable and well-preserved town of Zwettl, this Cistercian abbey has architecture dating from the Romanesque, Gothic and baroque periods. The church has a baroque tower and a richly decorative baroque interior, which includes a magnificent Gothic choir and 14-side chapels. The cloister, too, is highly elaborate, in both Romanesque and Gothic styles.

◆◆
## WALDVIERTEL

*Niederösterreich*

This area, on the border with the Czech Republic, is a part of Austria which deserves more attention from visitors. It was once heavily wooded, as its name suggests, and there is still some forest left. The region is suited to walkers or cyclists, but it also contains a large number of remarkable castles, monasteries and palaces (see above).

In the west the granite mountains often exceed 3,300 feet (1,000m), with Alpine forest, small lakes and moors. Small textile and glass industries have developed here. The climate is harsher than in the east, where sheep are grazed on a rolling plateau crossed by valleys. In all, this is a pleasant and unexploited corner of the country.

**Krems** and **Horn** (see separate entries) are good bases for exploring, but just as agreeable would be a stay west of Horn in the **Oberes Kamptal** (upper

Kamp valley), where man-made reservoirs such as Ottenstein offer many water sports. The valley itself has a fair quota of picturesque ruined castles, vineyards and arcaded houses. Two villages worth visiting on the Krems to Horn road are **Langenlois**, picturesque centre of the local wine trade, and **Gars am Kamp**, guarded by the ruins of its ancient fortress. **Retz**, to the northeast of the region, is a pretty walled town with 16th-century houses; it is also a major wine town (one of the main centres of the Weinviertel) and there are guided tours of the huge wine cellars.

**Tourist Office**
Waldviertel Region,
Gartenstrasse 3, A-3910 Zwettl
(tel: 2822-2414).

◆

### WEINVIERTEL

This area, sandwiched between northeast Vienna and the Czech and Slovak borders, gains its name from the extensive vineyards clothing its hillsides. The east has several oilfields. The chief reason for exploring this region is to visit some of the old wine cellars. However, there are also some towns of interest in which to while away some time between the tipples. **Mistelbach**, some 11 miles (18km) north of Vienna, has a 12th-century charnel house; its castle has a local museum. **Poysdorf**, in the north, has an early baroque Pfarrkirche (Parish Church) and Pestsäule (Plague Column). In **Laa an der Thaya**, near the Czech border, there is a beer museum in the

*A street of wine cellars, Poysdorf*

remains of a 13th-century castle, from which there are fine views. In **Hollabrunn**, on the western edge of the Weinviertel (northeast of Vienna), the Alte Hofmühle houses a local museum, sculptures and religious art. The town also has a Pestsäule, and a folk and wine festival in August.

To the southeast of Hollabrunn is **Stockerau**. The pastoral poet Nikolaus Lenau (1802–50) often stayed here, and there are performances of his works in summer.

On the north bank of the Danube, **Korneuburg** is home to the country's biggest shipyard. There is a good market here, as well as some fine old buildings.

**Tourist Office**
Weinviertel Region,
Liechtensteinstrasse 1, A-2170
Poysdorf (tel: 2552-3515).

## THE CENTRE

This chapter focuses on the northern province of Oberösterreich (Upper Austria), and much of Steiermark (Styria) and Kärnten (Carinthia). In the west it takes in most of Land Salzburg (Salzburg province).

The north has sharply defined areas. Linz, a major industrial and commercial city, and the Danube valley are rimmed by the isolated, forested Mühlviertel, which rolls on to the Bohemian border. To the south the Alpine hills gear up for that final push to become the eastern Alps. Everywhere there is a wealth of lovely old towns and abbeys.

Wealth is also the word to sum up exquisite Salzburg, one of the world's most beautiful cities. Rich architecturally, spiritually and intellectually, Salzburg is not to be missed.

To the east lies the popular Salzkammergut, a region of crystalline lakes and glimmering peaks.

The southern Carinthian lakes are absolutely gorgeous, but also crowded. This area spent much of its past fending off attacks from invaders such as the Turks, Hungarians and Slavs, resulting in a string of castles and fortifications ripe for exploring.

Any visit should include Austria's second city, Graz, full of vitality and interest.

Finally, there's music. Mozart may belong to Salzburg, but almost every town has a festival, and even the lake steamers have bands.

## WHAT TO SEE

◆◆
### BAD ISCHL
*Oberösterreich*

This attractive and elegant spa town, 11 miles (17km) southwest of the Traunsee, became popular after Emperor Franz-Josef made his summer home here in 1856. The **Kaiservilla** (Imperial Villa) is now a museum.

Royalty and treatments proved an irresistible lure to artists and intelligentsia. The composers Brahms, Bruckner and Franz Lehár are but a few of the famous who swarmed here. Lehár lives on – the **Lehár villa** can be visited and the annual operetta festival in July and August pays tribute to him.

The town's Biedermeier-style architecture reflects the royal influence. The **Café Zauner** (at Pfarrgasse 7) was frequented by the emperor and is still famous for its cakes.

The former salt-mines, the **Salzbergwerk**, are open for visits in summer. To the south of town is a cable car to the **Katrinalm**, for superb views.

*Keutschach's eye-catching ceramics*

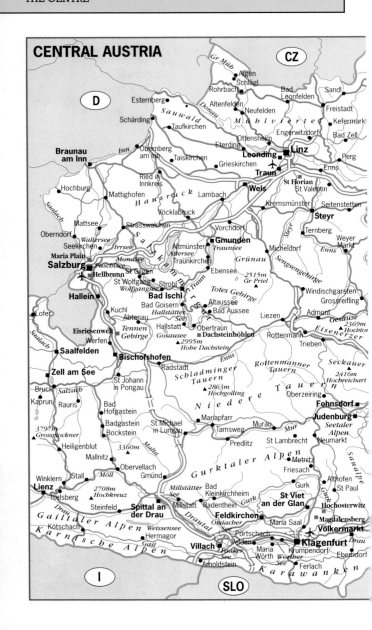

◆
## BAD KLEINKIRCHHEIM
*Kärnten*

A trendy summer and winter spa resort, situated at a height of 3,609 feet (1,100m). There are hot springs and several bathing complexes, including one which attempts to recreate Roman baths, with a Roman hot room. Even in winter it is possible to bathe in the open air, peering out through clouds of steam at fur-clad onlookers. There are lots of sports facilities, including an 18-hole golf course; and there are plenty of possibilities for gentle walks as well as hiking, with chair-lifts operating up neighbouring mountains. In season there are lively bars, and open-air concerts.

◆
## BRAUNAU AM INN
*Oberösterreich*

The birthplace of Adolf Hitler (1889–1945), this is a fine old town with well-preserved 16th- and 17th-century burghers' houses, a Gothic parish church with a 328-foot (100-m) tower, and remains of the medieval town walls – notably the Salzburger Tor (Salzburg Gate) in the impressive main square. There is a local museum in the old bell foundry in Johann Fischergasse.

### Excursions

Braunau is in the **Innviertel** (River Inn region) of Oberösterreich, a rich farming area full of pretty villages much like its German neighbour Bavaria. It is popular for cycling tours, and a network of cycle tracks has been established.

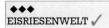

## ◆◆◆
## EISRIESENWELT

*Salzburg*

The 'World of the Ice Giants' is the name given to one of the world's largest accessible cave systems, high above the Salzach valley, in the Hochkogel mountain, part of the Tennengebirge range, 4 miles (6km) northeast of Werfen. The special thing here is that these are ice caverns, fairy-tale grottoes decorated by ice shapes – curtains, towers, figures – all formed by frozen water which trickles down through cracks in the rocks above. The whole trip from Werfen takes four to five hours, via 4 miles (6km) of unmade mountain road (bus and taxi available), cable car, and about 40 minutes walk to the entrance. The tour of the caves takes about two hours, and warm clothes, gloves and stout shoes are essential.

## ◆
## ENNS

*Oberösterreich*

On a river of the same name, 11 miles (17km) southeast of Linz, is Austria's oldest city. The Romans occupied it and recent excavations have found a Christian basilica dating from 370 AD. The town marked the border, after World War II, between the US and Soviet zones. Enns is an attractive place, dominated by the 16th-century **Stadtturm** (Town Tower) in the main square. The **Rathaus**, a mix of Gothic and baroque, has a town museum with Roman exhibits.

## ◆◆
## FREISTADT

*Oberösterreich*

This is the main town of the Mühlviertel (mill region). Once a medieval fort, a bulwark against the Bohemians to the north, Freistadt is one of the rare places to have perfectly preserved city walls. Indeed, the town has won a European prize for its preservation work, which can be seen in the **Linzer Tor** (Linz Gate).

In the **Hauptplatz** are fine soft-hued merchant houses from the 15th century. The **Pfarrkirche** (St Catherine's Church) has had a baroque overhaul. The Gothic **Schloss Freistadt** is now a local museum, with a good collection of decorated glass. This is a lovely, tranquil town. At night a watchman does the rounds calling 'Twelve o'clock and all's well!'

## Excursions

The Mühlviertel is a wooded region, little changed from medieval times, ideal for walking or fishing, and with reasonably priced accommodation. Towns include **Kefermarkt**, 7 miles (11km) southeast of Freistadt, with the huge 17th-century **Schloss Weinberg** and an extraordinary winged altar in the Gothic church; Bad Leonfelden, 12½ miles (20km) west of Freistadt), a very popular spa in summer; and the resort of Neufelden in the Grosse Mühl valley. Aigen, Schlägl and Rohrbach in the northwest, are other pleasant spots.

## ◆◆
## GMUNDEN
*Oberösterreich*

Gmunden's star as prosperous, well-to-do resort in the Salzkammergut (see separate entry) has never waned. Its picturesque position at the northern tip of the **Traunsee** – brimming with castles, and smiled on by mountains – certainly helps.

Gmunden's wealth came from nearby salt mines, and it retains its ambience of idle richness, more 19th rather than 20th century in style. Composers such as Mahler, Schubert and Brahms loved it, and the Biedermeier-style architecture is prominent.

A stroll along the promenade recalls more gentle days, but there are up-to-date water

*Gmunden – peaceful summer resort; an inspiration to artists and musicians then and now*

sports facilities all along the lake – including paragliding, rafting and sailing. To the southwest is the 17th-century **Schloss Ort**, on an island in the lake. One room has wall paintings by Gustav Klimt. On the main shore is a 'twin' building, linked by a bridge.

### Entertainment

Along the lakeside the tree-lined esplanade has concerts in summer. Recently, Gmunden has acquired a festival (mid-August to September) attracting international musicians. There is an attractive old-fashioned theatre, and the Rathaus is also used for performances.

## Shopping

The famous product of Gmunden is the pottery of the Keramikfabrik, with its distinctive green swirls and curlicues on a white base. The factory in Keramikstrasse 24 sells seconds, as well as many other hand-painted designs. Tours of the factory take place at 09.30hrs on Tuesdays and Thursdays in July and August. In late August, there's a pottery festival.

## Accommodation and Restaurants

The newly refurbished four-star **Seehotel Schwan**, Rathausplatz 8 (tel: 7612-3391) is on the lake; it has a large café with an outside terrace, where one can eat modestly and well. **Hotel Freisitz Roith**, Traunsteinstrasse 87 (tel: 7612-66081) on the opposite shore is another very attractive four-star hotel. The three-star **Hotel Magerl**, Ackerweg 81 (tel: 7612-3675) is family run, with a rural aspect. Two reasonably priced hotels are **Pension Hammerschmid**, Traunsteinstrasse 141 (tel: 7612-3692), in a beautiful location on the waterside, and **Pension Alpensee**, Traunsteinstrasse 44 (tel: 7612-4352), also in a lovely spot. Chalets and flats are available, but camping is forbidden. The **Toscana Café** is in a glamorous setting: an Italian-style villa by the lake in Toscanapark.

## Excursions

In summer the **Traunsee** is criss-crossed by ships, including one said to be one of the oldest of its kind in the world, the antique steamer Gisela (information from the Traunschiffahrt Eder office opposite the Rathaus; tel: 7612-5215).

There are many good walks from Gmunden; on Thursdays there's a guided tour (tel: 7612-4305). A good half-day walk is Gmunden-Landachsee to Franzl im Holz and back to Gmunden. For mountain hikes, information is available from the Alpenschule Salzkammergut (tel: 7612-5208). You can take a cable car up the **Grünberg** for fine views of the lake and the Dachstein glacier.

## Tourist Office

Kurverwaltung Gmunden, Am Graben 2, A-4810 Gmunden. (tel: 7612-4305).

### ◆◆◆
### GRAZ ✓

*Styria*

Visitors tend to bypass Graz, the capital of Steiermark (Styria), even though it is Austria's second city. That is quite a mistake because it is a really interesting and enjoyable town. The essential ingredients are there: a palace, ruined fortress, medieval and baroque architecture, and one of the largest 'old towns' in Europe. Add to this two universities, a music academy, several parks, much industry, and a welter of history and culture, all of which has percolated through to create a lively contemporary

*Graz – unique, ancient and vibrant*

scene that firmly puts paid to Graz's former image as a rather stuffy place fit only for retirement. Graz lies on the River Mur, in a natural basin, bounded by the Alps to the north. To the northwest of the centre lies the Schlossberg on an outcrop of rock that has proved to be strategically useful over the centuries. The Habsburgs developed the city's potential, promoting its status until it became an imperial seat in the 14th to 17th centuries; many superb Italianate buildings were constructed during their rule, and the city's wealth increased from its silver and iron industries.

Unnerved by the Protestant surge, the Habsburgs built many churches and welcomed the Jesuits. Both factions encouraged learning, and Graz established its reputation as a seat of academic excellence. The city stood firm against the Turks for almost 200 years, a source of much civic pride (although it later fell to Napoleon). After the court moved to Vienna, Graz flourished again in the 19th century under the ruler Archduke Johann, a lover of the arts and sciences. Today the city still has a vibrant cultural life.

### Sightseeing

#### Altstadt

The compact old town of Graz lies on the east bank of the River Mur. In the Hauptplatz stands the **Erzherzog Johann Brunnen** (Archduke Johann Fountain), in memory of the well-loved ruler; also here is the late

## THE CENTRE

19th century **Rathaus** (Town Hall) and, on the corner of Sporgasse, the **Haus Luegg,** distinguished by arcades and baroque stucco work.

Just to the west by the Hauptbrücke is the Gothic **Franziskanerkirche** (Franciscan Church), surrounded by narrow medieval streets.

In Neutorgasse lies the main part of the **Landesmuseum Joanneum**, one of the best provincial museums in Europe, containing magnificent collections of medieval and baroque art, including works by Cranach and Brueghel, as well as musical instruments, ironwork, costumes, and furniture.

In the pedestrianised Herrengasse are fine town mansions, such as no 3, the **Gemaltes Haus** (Painted House), with 18th-century frescos.

The remarkable Renaissance **Landhaus** (1557–67), now home to the provincial council, was built by the Italian Domenico dell'Alio, and has tiers of arcades, fine Styrian wrought iron work, and an ornate stucco hall.

Next door is one of Europe's most fascinating buildings, testimony to the city's role as bastion against the Turks. The **Landes-Zeughaus** (Provincial Arsenal) is unique. It was built in 1642 and remains largely unaltered, packed with 30,000 weapons and armour from the 16th and 17th centuries.

To the east of the Landhaus, the carillon in **Glockenspielplatz** puts on a lively little show at 11.00hrs and 18.00hrs each day, as a troupe of wooden figures pirouette to folk music. The courtyards behind the houses here merit a look, for their Renaissance arcades and (at no 5) a 17th-century staircase.

The imposing 15th-century **Domkirche** (Cathedral) has a decorated doorway and a faded Gothic fresco telling of Graz's past adversaries: the Turks, plague, and locusts. More lavish is the mausoleum of the 17th-century Emperor Ferdinand.

Just north are the vestiges of the **Burg**, the old imperial palace, much altered and now serving as offices, but with an eye-catching double-helix stone staircase, fused in the middle and apparently unsupported. Along Hofgasse northeast to the Schlossburg is the **Herberstein Palace**, now the **Neue Galerie** (New Gallery), which has a good collection of 19th- and 20th-century art, with several works by Schiele and contemporary Styrian pieces.

### Schlossberg

A funicular goes to the top of the Schlossberg (otherwise it is a steepish 30-minute climb). The ramparts, extended to ward off the Turks heading for Vienna, were dismantled by a victorious Napoleon. The city paid his ransom demands to save the 115-foot (35-m) **Glockenturm** (belfry), with its four-ton 'Liesl' bell. Also ransomed was the huge four-faced **Uhrturm** (Clock Tower), Graz's landmark, at the south end of the hill, built so the time could be read across the city.

### Schloss Eggenberg

On the west side of the Mur, 2 miles (3km) from the centre, this baroque, arcaded palace has fine state rooms. The **Prunksaal**, now used for candlelit concerts, has rich stucco decoration. There are also an art collection, hunting museum, and prehistoric exhibits. A deer park surrounds the *Schloss*, and there is a nice café.

### Entertainment

The Stadtpark has a fine opera house, with a thriving season. Graz is also well known for jazz. There's a theatre near the cathedral, and an open-air theatre by the belfry on Schlossberg, plus several smaller ones for fringe events. The Autumn Festival (Steirischer Herbst) brings all the avant-garde together in a multi-media extravaganza.

### Accommodation and Restaurants

Being a sizeable town, there are all kinds of hotels. By the Mur facing the old town are the five-star **Grand Hotel Wiesler**, Grieskai 4–8 (tel: 316-90660)

*Step back 300 years at the perfectly preserved Arsenal*

and four-star **Hotel Das Weitzer**, Grieskai 12–14 (tel: 316-9030). The two-star **Hotel Zur Stadt Feldbach**, is centrally located in Hötzendorfstrasse 58 (tel: 316-829468).

In the **Landhaus** building, the café serves excellent Styrian cuisine in the memorable setting of the superb courtyard. At **Schmiedgasse** 9 there has been an inn for 400 years, serving Styrian wine and beer. Graz is one of the cities priding itself on its *Bermuda Dreieck* (Bermuda Triangle), an area with so many bars and pubs it is possible to enter and disappear forever. Here, in the central old town, try **Kastello**, in Trautmannsdortgasse 3, **Altstadtbeisl** at Mehlplatz 1, or **Haring** at Mehlplatz 4.

Good cafés include **Hof Café**, Hofgasse; **Café Glockenspiel**, Glockenspielplatz; and **Kaiserhof**, Kaiserfeldgasse. A local culinary speciality is the dark green *Kürbiskernöl* (pumpkinseed oil), which is used in salads.

*A dramatic setting for Hallstatt*

### Excursions

At Piber, 27 miles (40km) west of Graz, is the **Lipizzaner Gestüt** (Stud), where the white stallions for the Viennese Spanish Riding School are reared. It is possible to view the stables.

Nine miles (15km) northwest of Graz, **Stübing** is the site of the **Österreichisches Freilichtmuseum** (Austrian Open-air Museum). Here is a fascinating collection of rural buildings, huts, windmills and farms from all over Austria, dating from the 16th century to the present day. Craftsmen can be seen at work.

To the south of Graz is attractive wine country, known locally as **'Styrian Tuscany'**. **Leibnitz** is the main centre; a good place at which to buy and taste wine is **Ehrenhausen**, where the inns are called *Buschenschänke* and serve a light rosé wine called Schilcher.

### ◆◆◆ HALLSTATT ✓

*Oberösterreich*

This small and pretty town on Hallstätter See in the Salzkammergut (see separate entry) is huddled at the foot of the steep Salzberg, which rises sheer from the water's edge to make a very picturesque setting, and frames the town's large 15th-century **Pfarrkirche**. It is overlooked by the Krippenstein, at 6,919 feet (2,109m) a mere foothill of the 9,826-foot (2,995-m) Hoher Dachstein behind.

Hallstatt's salt mines are reputed to be the oldest anywhere, so productive that the town gave its name to a period in the Iron Age. Their history is explained in the interesting local **museum of prehistory**.

Another sight of particular interest in Hallstatt, although probably only to hardier mortals, is the **Beinhaus**

(Charnel House). The cemetry, like the rest of the steeply terraced town, suffers from lack of space, so skulls and bones are removed to make way for new burials, and placed in the charnel house where they can be gazed at.

On a jollier note, 30 May is the Corpus Christi Festival, with water processions, and decorations on the lake boats.

### Accommodation and Restaurants

The four-star **Seehotel Grüner Baum**, (tel: 6134-8263) is on the old market square, and has a lake terrace. Inexpensive **Gasthof Simony**, Wolfengasse 105 (tel: 6134-8231) is an old building near the lake. Bed and breakfast is available at several private houses, including **Helga Lenz**, Hallberg 17(tel: 6134-8508).

A pleasant restaurant is **Gasthof Strandcafé**, Seelände 102, has a lakeside location near the beach, and garden facilities.

### Excursions

The **salt mines** offer a guided tour in summer. To reach them, take a funicular from nearby Lahn to Rudolfsturm, where there are ruins of fortifications used to protect the wealth of the mines. Canals used to carry the salt in solution to be processed at Ebensee.

**Obertraun**, 3 miles (4km) east, is the start of a trip to the **Dachsteineishöhle**, the Dachstein Ice Cave. This involves taking a cable car to **Schönbergalpe**, and then walking to the huge and bizarre caverns, full of giant stalactites and stalagmites, and featuring a frozen waterfall in the Giant Cavern. Tours last almost two hours – it's important to wrap up well and wear stout shoes. Northeast of Hallstatt is the spa of **Bad Aussee**, which has attractive 15th-century houses and lovely walks. Even nicer is **Altaussee** further north: a tiny lake and village, unspoiled and quite magical. In World War II the Germans stored priceless art treasures in salt mines just west of here.

About 11 miles (17km) west of the Hallstätter See, **Gosausee** is a beautiful and quiet mountain lake, superbly situated for hiking.

### KLAGENFURT

*Kärnten*

The capital of the province of Carinthia, Klagenfurt was a low-key market town until the 16th century, when it began to expand to become the commercial centre it is today. The Altstadt (Old Town) has many fine pastel-hued buildings and courtyards from all periods, baroque to art nouveau, beautifully restored and maintained. Particularly impressive are those in the Alter Platz, including the arcaded 17th-century **Rathaus**, and the 16th-century **Goldene Gans** (Golden Goose) house. The finest is probably the domed 16th-century **Landhaus**, with an arcaded courtyard and a Heraldic Hall (Grosser Wappensaal) which is distinguished by *trompe l'oeil* and over 600 coats of arms. Just to the north of Alter Platz, **Wienergasse** also has many picturesque houses, several sporting stucco animals' heads. At the edge of the pedestrian precinct, in **Neuer Platz**, is the famous and much photographed stone fountain which features the city's emblem, a fearsome dragon (*Lindwurm*).

### Entertainment

The **Stadttheater**, near the Landhaus, built in the *Jugendstil* (art nouveau) style, has a season of opera, operetta and plays, and occasional ballet and concerts. In summer much use is made of the many beautiful courtyards for performances.

### Accommodation and Restaurants

Klagenfurt boasts a couple of glamourous hotels, both in old palaces: the **Romantik Hotel Musil**, 10-Oktoberstrasse 14 (tel: 463-511660) and the **Schlosshotel Palais Porcia**, Neuer Platz 13 (tel: 463-511590). There are also plenty of more modest establishments. The **Hotel Moser-Verdino**, Domgasse 2 (tel: 463-57878), is in an Art Nouveau building, and has a café and cocktail bar. The three-star **Blumenstöckl** is centrally located at 10-Oktoberstrasse 11 (tel: 463-57793). Also see **Wörther See**, page 69.

### Excursions

**St Veit an der Glan**, 11 miles (18km) northeast, has very attractive baroque buildings – particularly the **Rathaus**, which has a courtyard decorated with sgraffito.

### LINZ

*Oberösterreich*

Austria's third city and capital of Upper Austria, Linz has worked hard to change its image. Once a polluted, industrial Danube port, Linz was heavily bombed in World War II, but was rebuilt at record speed. Now the city is pristine and interesting, a place where the iron, steel and chemical industries blend with a brisk commercial and cultural life. In September, the area between Linz and St Florian erupts with a galaxy of events to celebrate the International Bruckner Festival in memory of the composer.

Linz has a number of fine old buildings, particularly in Hauptplatz and Altstadt, and several churches of interest. The main sights for the visitor, however, are an especially rich **Landesmuseum** (provincial museum), housed in the *Schloss* overlooking the Danube; and a good modern art gallery: the **Neue Galerie**, in Blütenstrasse, Urfahr (on the left bank), which includes works by Klimt and Kokoschka.

### Entertainment

The Brucknerhaus, opened in 1974, houses the annual Bruckner Festival, which includes experimental music. Tickets are available from Untere Donaulände 7, A-4010 Linz, (tel: 732-275230). The Linz Opera is highly regarded, and puts on a season at the Landestheater. Linz also has a name for avant-garde theatre productions. There is a casino in the Schillerpark Hotel.

## Accommodation and Restaurants

The five-star **Hotel Schillerpark**, Rainerstrasse 2–4 (tel: 732-6950103) has a casino, a no-smoking floor, and water-beds on request. More atmospheric is the four-star **Domhotel**, at Baumbachstrasse 17, near the cathedral (tel: 732-778441). In a nice old building in Graben 24–6, the three-star family hotel **Mühlviertlerhof** (tel: 732-772268) has a well-regarded French restaurant. The 2-star **Wienerwald**, in Freinbergstrasse 18 (tel: 732-777881), is in a quiet rustic building with fine views. The youth hostel is very pleasant and central, at Kapuzinerstrasse 14 (tel: 782-782720).

## Tourist Office

Städtische Fremdenverkehrszentrale, Hauptplatz 34, Altstadt 17, A-4010 Linz (tel: 732-2393).

*Exquisite ceiling frescos decorate the Abbey of St Florian. You may hear world-class concerts here in season.*

## Excursions

The **Abbey of St Florian**, 9½ miles (15km) southeast of Linz, is not to be missed. This magnificent Augustinian monastery, founded in the 11th century, dominates the small town of St Florian and the countryside around. It was rebuilt between 1686 and 1751 by Carlone and Prandtauer, and is considered one of Austria's most magnificent baroque church buildings. The abbey church has almost supernatural dimensions, and almost everything is encrusted in elaborate stucco, or exquisitely carved, including the black marble pulpit. Anton Bruckner, who was organist here, is buried in the crypt. Other things of note include an eagle fountain in the couryard, Albrecht Altdorfer's vivid St Sebastian altarpiece in the gallery, and the magnificent library, with ceiling frescos by Altomonte. After all the visual excesses, the Stiftkeller provides welcome refreshment of a more down to earth nature.

## THE CENTRE

## MARIAZELL
*Styria*

The basilica of Mariazell, the most popular of all Austrian pilgrimage centres, lies amid superb mountain scenery at the eastern edge of the Alps. The Benedictines came in 1157 but Mariazell gained fame as a place for miracles when Louis I, the Hungarian king, believed the Virgin had helped his triumph over the Turks. This faith is embodied in a 12th-century statue, the Virgin of Mariazell, in the Gnadenkapelle (Miracles Chapel) of the 14th-century basilica, enlarged in the mid-1600s. Points of interest here include the Tympanum (1438), ornate stucco decoration, and a high altar by baroque master Fischer von Erlach, in the form of a silver globe. The treasury, with centuries of offerings, is splendid too.

There is a steam railway from Mariazell to **Erlaufsee**, a pretty lake a couple of miles (3km) northwest, and a cable car goes up to the **Bürgeralpe**, 4,022 feet (1,226m), from where there are very good walks.

---

### Mountains and Valleys

For those who enjoy the challenge and inspiration of driving in the mountains, four scenic routes are suggested:

● **Mariazell to Hieflau** This route follows the Salza ravine, through forested and increasingly wild countryside, virtually uninhabited. From

● **Brunn**, there are particularly fine views of the Hochschwab massif to the south. The section of road between Palfau and Grossreifling is very steep and winding.

● **Liezen to Hieflau** This is another ravine route, along the bottom of the steep walls of the dramatic Gesäuse, which can best be viewed from just to the east of Admont, where the Benedictine Abbey has a famous rococo library.

● **Hieflau to Leoben** This route crosses the Erzberg, the Iron Mountain, has been mined since Roman times and was the major provider of wealth for the former Austrian Empire. The Leopoldsteiner See, a small detour to the east, is a small deep emerald green lake surrounded by sheer cliffs. Eisenerz, a medieval mining town, is at the foot of the Erzberg; from here the road climbs steeply to Präbichl Pass (4,041 feet, 1,232m). The scenery south to Leoben is agreeably alpine, halted abruptly by the steelworks.

● **Judenberg to Trieben** The road across the Hohentauern Pass (4,150 feet, 1,265m), demands great care, particularly on the stretch just to the north of the pass which has gradients greater than 1 in 8 as the road descends into the dark gorge of the Wolfsgraben. The southern part of the road passes derelict buildings from the time when this was a thriving centre for silver mining. A small detour takes you to the former mining village of Oberzeiring where you can visit a silver mine.

*Salzburg – an architectural delight*

### ◆◆◆

In Salzburg man and nature
found a divine complicity to
work a magic few mortals can
resist. The grandeur of the
mountain backdrop serves to
heighten the city's architectural
majesty, and there's music and
Mozart too. However, one soon
comes to realise that more
material concerns have created
this city, such as the alliance of
power, politics and religion. The
huge medieval fortress is as
much a symbol of these as is the
beauty of the city's churches
and palaces.

For the visitor this is less
relevant, although it may help
offset the vague feeling that at
times Salzburg is a little too
perfect. The large summer
crowds (particularly during
Salzburg's international music
festival in July and August) and
dreadful parking problems
unfortunately inject a dose of
reality, too. Whatever the
season, however, visual and
aural harmony are intrinsic to
the city, making Salzburg
unforgettable.

**History**
Salzburg's position made it ripe
for settlement from Celtic times:
on the river Salzach at a natural
crossroads for trading routes,
and near mineral wealth (*Salz*
means `salt'). The Romans called
it *Juvavum* (Home of the Sky God)
promoting it to a chief town; and
indeed today the city is more like
a capital than a provincial seat.
After the Barbarians ransacked
and abandoned it, Salzburg rose
again when the Christians took
over in the 7th century, and it
became a bishopric. From then
on centuries of enterprising
archbishops made it what it is
today.

The Romanesque period saw
much building, but it was really
in the 12th to 15th centuries that

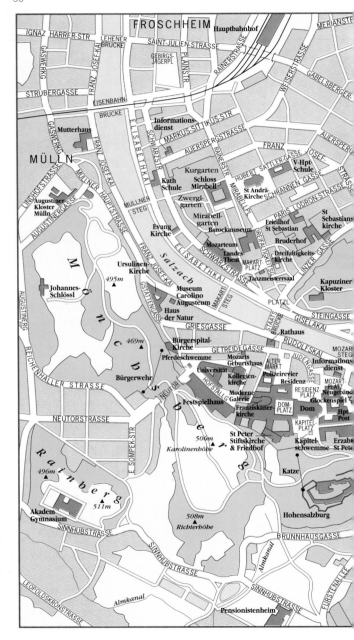

FROSCHHEIM

IGNAZ HARRER-STR · LEHENER BRÜCKE · SAINT-JULIEN-STRASSE · Hauptbahnhof · MERIANSTR
GEBIRGS-JÄGERPL · PLAINSTR · RAINERSTRASSE · WESERSTRASSE · GABELSBERGER
GASWERKG · STRUBERGASSE · FRANZ JOSEF-KAI
EISENBAHN-BRÜCKE
Informations-dienst
MÜLLN
Mutterhaus
MARKUS SITTIKUS-STR · SCHWARZSTR · ELISABETHKAI
AUERSPERGSTRASSE · RAINERSTR · AUERSPERG
FRANZ · HUBERT SATTLER-GASSE · JOSEF- · STR
V.-Hpt.-Schule
GASWERKG · LINDHOFSTRASSE · MÜLLNER KAI · MÜLLNER HAUPTSTRASSE · AUGUSTINERGASSE
Kath Schule · Kurgarten · Schloss Mirabell · SCHRANNEN GASSE · St Andrä-Kirche
Zwergl-garten · MIRABELLPL · PARIS LODRON-STRASSE
Augustiner-Kloster Mülln · MÜLLNER STEG
Evang Kirche · Mirabell-garten · Barockmuseum · Friedhof St Sebastian · St Sebastians-kirche
ELISABETHKAI · Mozarteum · DREIFALTIGKEITS · Bruderhof · LINZER GASSE
Landes-Theat · Dreifaltigkeits-kirche
Ursulinen-Kirche · 495m · SCHWARZSTRASSE · MAKART-PLATZ · Tanzmeistersaal
Kapuziner Kloster
M · Ö · Johannes-Schlössl · FRANZ JOSEF-KAI · Salzach
Museum Carolino Augusteum · MAKART STEG · PLATZL · STEINGASSE
Haus der Natur · STATS BRÜCKE
GRIESGASSE · GISELAKAI
AUGUSTINERG · n · c · 469m · Bürgerspital-Kirche · GETREIDEGASSE · Rathaus · RUDOLFSKAI · MOZART STEG
Pferdeschwemme · Mozarts Geburtshaus · ALTER MARKT · JUDENGASSE · Informations-dienst
REICHENHALLER STRASSE · Bürgerwehr · h · s · Universität · Polizeirevier · MOZART-PLATZ
Kollegien-kirche · Residenz · Neugebäu
NEUTORSTRASSE · NEUTOR · E SOMPEK-STR · HOFSTALLG · Moderne Galerie · RESIDENZ PLATZ · Glockenspiel
Festspielhaus · Franziskaner-kirche · DOM-PLATZ · Dom · Hpt Post
St Peter · KAPITEL-PLATZ
R · a · 506m · Stiftskirche & Friedhof · Kapitel-schwemme · Erzab St Pete
i · Karolinenhöhe · n · b · e · Katze
496m · r · g · 511m
Akadem Gymnasium · SINNHUBSTRASSE · 508m · Richterhöhe · Hohensalzburg
BRUNNHAUSGASSE
LEOPOLDSKRONSTRASSE · SINNHUBSTRASSE · Almkanal · FÜRSTENALLEE
Almkanal · SINNHUBSTRASSE · Pensionistenheim

**THE CENTRE**

the power lines of money, religion and the arts all came together in one great surge. The baroque period was the icing on the cake. Under Archbishop Wolf Dietrich von Raitenau (1578–1612), a great admirer of the Italian Renaissance, Salzburg was shaped into many squares and courtyards. Between him and his successor, Markus Sittikus, the cathedral was built, and then completed by Paris Count Lodron whose defensive constructions saved Salzburg from the ravages of the Thirty Years' War (1618–1648). Archbishop Johann Ernst von Thun (1687–1709) promoted the architect Johann Bernhard Fischer von Erlach whose baroque masterpieces are the finest anywhere.

The harmony of styles was perpetuated by architect Johann Lukas von Hildebrandt in the early 18th century. In the 19th century, Salzburg's star waned, but in a sense Mozart's genius revived it, and Salzburg became famed for its music and a repository of high culture.

*The lovely Mirabell Gardens*

# THE CENTRE

## Sightseeing

The city falls roughly into three areas: the Altstadt (Old Town) on the west bank beneath the Mönchsberg ridge and the river; the right bank, an interesting mixture of medieval workers' streets, a gorgeous palace, and contemporary arts studios; and the Hohensalzburg fortress area. The main tourist office is in Mozartplatz in the Altstadt.

## Altstadt

In the Residenzplatz is the grand **Residenz** (Bishops' Palace), built around three courtyards, with a huge baroque fountain. The state rooms are full of riches. There is a guided tour taking in the Rittersaal (Knights' Hall) where concerts are held. In the Residenzgalerie are art collections including works by Rembrandt and Rubens. From the **Neugebäude**, the former Archbishops' Guesthouse, the tower carillon (*Glockenspiel*) trills out Mozart at 07.00, 11.00 and 18.00hrs daily. A roaring response comes from the 'bull' organ in the fortress.

In Domplatz is the twin-towered **Dom** (St Rupert's Cathedral), the first Italianate church in northern Europe. Recently restored after heavy shelling in World War II, it is adorned with pink Salzburg marble; the bronze doors are modern. The cathedral **treasury** and **Kunst- und Wunderkammer** (Chamber of Art and Rarities) contain many fine and curious pieces.

Also in the square is the **Mariensäule** (Virgin Column). The *Jedermann* (Everyman) play by Hugo von Hofmannsthal is performed here annually during the festival.

Kapitelplatz has the Benedictine **Erzabtei St Peter** (St Peter's Monastery and Abbey). The site dates from 690 but the present church is a Romanesque basilica converted to late baroque, one of the finest in Salzburg, with a

*Enjoy Salzburg's dramatic backdrop from Café Winkler*

15th-century Madonna, rococo decoration and altar paintings by 'Kremser' Schmidt. The **Friedhof** (cemetery) has many famous names, including Mozart's sister 'Nannerl'. It backs on to the rock wall of the Mönchsberg where there are Christian catacombs and a chapel cut from the rock face.
The **Franziskanerkirche** (Franciscan Church) is perhaps the city's most interesting one. Dating from the 8th century, it has Romanesque, late-Gothic, Renaissance and baroque features – a condensed version of the city itself. The marble altar and baroque chapels are superb.
In Wiener-Philharmoniker-Gasse is the **Rupertinum**, now a 20th-century art museum, with many works by Kokoschka and Schiele.
The **Festspielhäuser** (Festival Halls) are just to the northwest. One was originally the old court stables, with designs by Fischer von Erlach. The old festival hall, called the Mozart, has statues of great conductors and a tapestry by Oskar Kokoschka. The larger one, called the Wagner, was built in the late 1950s and has a massive stage hacked out of the Mönchsberg; its acoustics are said to be unrivalled. Fountains and sculptures, ornate painted theatre boxes and busts of musicians form a backdrop for major operas and concerts. The festival was founded in 1920 by Hugo von Hofmannsthal, and has an international reputation.
The **Kollegienkirche** (Collegiate Church), opposite the Festival Halls, is Fischer von Erlach's finest and biggest Salzburg church, with a lovely convex façade and turrets. Further north, in Sigmundsplatz, is the 17th-century **Marstallschwemme**, a trough where horses were washed; it has a decorated wall and sculptures.
The old town district near the river is highly attractive, with wrought iron work and 15th- to 18th-century merchants' houses. Mozart was born at **no 9 Getreidegasse**, one of the oldest roads in town, and the museum here is thoughtfully laid out with domestic momentoes as well as an exhibition explaining Mozart's role in the theatre.
To the west, in Museumsplatz, the **Museum Carolino Augusteum** has a superb collection of decorative arts from the 15th century to the present day.

### Right Bank
Formerly where workers and artisans lived, this area is still favoured by present-day artists. Despite being called the `newer' part of town, some of it dates from the 14th century.
In Linzergasse is the **Sebastianskirche** (St Sebastian's Church), an elaborate rococo remodelling. Mozart's father and his widow Konstanze are buried in the cemetery.
**Steinergasse** has interesting shops, studios and clubs; it was the birthplace of Josef Mohr, who wrote the *Stille Nacht* carol, and also has the Max Reinhardt Institute, devoted to the work of the theatre director. Beyond is the Kapuzinerkloster

(Capuchin Friary) on the wooded **Kapuzinerberg**, which has excellent views of the city. Down the hill leads to the Makartplatz area where there is another Fischer von Erlach creation, the baroque **Dreifaltigkeitskirche** (Trinity Church); and the **Mozart Wohnhaus** (Mozart's family house), a one-room museum of relatively little interest.

The **Schloss Mirabell**, to the northwest of Makartplatz, was the elaborate gift of Archbishop Wolf Dietrich in 1606 to his mistress Salome Alt; it was built in baroque style by Lukas von Hildebrandt. The Marmorsaal (Marble Hall) is used for concerts and civil ceremonies. The superb formal gardens with beautiful statues and fountains, contain an orangery which houses a museum devoted to the baroque period, and a Zwerglgarten (Dwarves' Garden).

### Hohensalzburg and Nonnberg

The medieval fortress – the largest preserved fortress in central Europe – dominates the city; it can be reached by a steep 20-minute walk, or by funicular from Festungsgasse. Guided tours of the interior cover rich Gothic apartments; there are two small museums, one with a torture chamber. To the east is the Benedictine convent of **Nonnberg**. Its main claim to fame is that it was the convent of Maria von Trapp (both in real life, and in the film of her life, *The Sound of Music*). You can still hear nuns singing in the attractive old convent church.

### Shopping

Salzburg is a very chic city, and shopping is excellent. In the old town, Judengasse and Getreidegasse, and the arcades beside them, are the streets for window shopping. Linzergasse is better for more practical shopping. Specialities include Austrian hats, lederhosen and loden coats, beeswax and honey products, and a wide range of Mozart-inspired souvenirs, notably the chocolates called Mozartkugeln. Markets (*Schranne*) are held on Thursdays around the St Andrä Church, and Grünmarkt operates daily on Universitätsplatz.

### Entertainment

Salzburg is above everything a musical city, as far as events are concerned. Mozart dominates the calendar, but not to the exclusion of other composers.

The world-famous **Salzburg Festival** in July and August is the highlight, but at Easter there is a festival of opera too. Early booking for both is advised. Applications can be made to Salzburger Festspiele, Hofstallgasse 1, A-5020 Salzburg (tel: 662-846500).

Concerts are held regularly at the Schloss Mirabell, the Residenz, the Fortress, and the Mozarteum. It is also worth reading the notices pinned on main church doors for details of free concerts.

The **Marionetten Theater**, in Schwarzstrasse, is a wonderful place for people of all ages: a puppet theatre which stages plays and operas (with a soundtrack).

## Accommodation and Restaurants

The five-star **Goldener Hirsch**, Getreidegasse 37 (tel: 662-848511) is the most famous old hostelry, baronial in style. Similar is the **Schloss Mönchstein**, Am Mönchsberg 26 (tel: 662-8485550), in wooded grounds high above the old town. More modest but well placed options are the four-star **Kasererbräu**, Kaigasse 33 (tel: 662-8424450) and the **Elefant**, Sigmund Haffner Gasse 4 (tel: 662-843397). Salzburg is full of delightful cafés and restaurants. The elegant **Café Winkler** at the top of the Mönchsberg is renowned for its night views and for good food. The 18th-century **Café Tomaselli** is well placed in the heart of the old town, at Alter Markt 9. A typical Salzburg restaurant is the beer garden or cellar: a popular one is the **Stiftskeller St Peter**, found opposite the church.

## Getting Around

Salzburg is compact and easily covered on foot. Parking a car is difficult but, bicycles can be hired. Bus tickets are cheaper bought in blocks (from kiosks or the tourist office) than singly; there's a one-day tourist ticket which includes the funicular and lift up the Mönchsberg. *Fiaker* (pony traps) are fun for children; they are based in Residenzplatz.

Lots of operators organise tours; the main city one is the 'Sound of Music' tour, which covers the city and its surroundings, with appropriate musical accompaniment.

*Tired of chess? – tired of life! A real-life game in the centre of Salzburg*

## Wolfgang Amadeus Mozart

Mozart, considered by many to have been the greatest musical genius the world has seen, was born in Salzburg in 1756 to a musical family. His father's treatise on violin playing is still respected to this day. An infant prodigy, Mozart's childhood was spent touring the centres of European culture and playing to court audiences. Wolfgang would perform with his sister Nannerl and could play anything on sight or by ear, without looking at the keyboard. He also learned to play the viola without being taught.

As an adult, he would write out whole scores while chatting to his friends at the same time.

Mozart eventually settled in Vienna, which he described as 'the right place for a man of my metier'. He was a lively and earthy letter-writer and so we know a fair bit about his daily life, including such details as the fact that his favourite dinner was the Salzburg speciality of *Leberknödel mit Sauerkraut.* Mozart's output was prodigious (he died at the age of 35), consisting of orchestral and instrumental works, piano music, religious masses, songs and operas. He was the first composer to explore the dramatic potential of opera: one example of this is that he wrote pieces in which six singers all sing at once while furthering the development of the plot, which had never been done before.

### Tourist Office

Fremdenverkehrsbetriebe der Stadt Salzburg, Auerspergstrasse 7, A- 5020 Salzburg (tel: 662-889870).

### Excursions

**Schloss Hellbrunn**, 4 miles (6km) south of Salzburg, is where the archbishops went to have fun. Built in the early 17th century, the Italianate interior, though fine, is less interesting than the gardens, where brilliant trick fountains spurt water from all angles, and give great delight to children and practical jokers. There is also a folklore museum and a zoo here.

Another 4 miles (6km) southwest of Hellbrunn is the **Untersberg**, with cable car. **Hallein**, 10 miles (16km) south of the city has the **Dürrnberg salt mines** near by; guided tours are available.

Three miles (5km) north of Salzburg is the striking baroque pilgrimage church of **Maria Plain**. About 9 miles (15km) northwest of here is **Oberndorf** village where organist Franz Gruber put music to the words of the carol *Stille Nacht*, (*Silent Night*); there is a memorial chapel.

◆◆

## SALZKAMMERGUT

This beautiful hilly area to the east of Salzburg, sprinkled with glacial lakes, is extremely popular. There is little public transport, but coaches and cars descend at weekends, and hotels and campsites fill with visitors who come to enjoy the ample sports facilities,

*Steyr has many attractive features*

abundance of good (and often expensive) restaurants, and beaches. During the Salzburg Festival, the area also serves as a base for those who prefer to commute into the city.

The name Salzkammergut means `salt chamber estate', reflecting the local industry of salt mining from which the crown drew its wealth. Salt (the word salary comes from the Latin word for salt ration) was used by soldiers as a means of barter.

Highlights include:

● **Attersee**, the largest of the Austrian lakes (apart from Neusiedler See), and the quietest in the Salzkammergut, is lined with orchards, and views take in the Höllen mountains in the west. Both Mahler and the painter Klimt loved to stay there.

● **Fuschlsee**, one of the loveliest and smallest of the lakes, is also the warmest.

● **Mondsee**, overlooked by the Schafberg, is a very picturesque lake with a pleasant village, whose parish church featured in the film *The Sound of Music*.

● **Traunsee**, one of the largest lakes, is warm despite being the deepest, with lovely views. It was near the village of Traunkirchen that Wagner composed part of *Tristan and Isolde*.

● **Wolfgang See** gets very crowded in summer. The cable car ride up the Zwolferhorn is recommended. The resort of St Wolfgang is very picturesque. Strobl, at the eastern end, and St Gilgen, in the west, are quieter and more sedate.

## STEYR
*Oberösterreich*

A very beautiful market town, at the confluence of the Steyr and Enns rivers, Steyr has managed to preserve its Gothic beauty as well as develop its modern car industry. The city's wealth originated from the iron ore in the Eisenerz mountains to the south.

Despite a fire which ravaged the town in the 18th century, the old town with gabled, red-tiled roofs still keeps its medieval aspect. Particularly attractive buildings include the **Schnallentor**, with elaborate sgraffito work, the **Rathaus**, and the Gothic **Bummerlhaus**, now a bank, in the glorious Stadtplatz. The town museum, in a 17th-century granary, is another building to display sgraffito work. Appropriate to Steyr's car-production role, there is an interesting **Museum der Arbeitswelt** (Industrial Museum). Just to the west of town is the village of **Christkindl** (Christ Child), which has set up a special post office to send children's letters to Santa Claus and festive greetings to stamp collectors worldwide.

### Accommodation and Restaurants

The four-star **Hotel Minichmayr** is in the `Romantik' group, and is located at the meeting point of the rivers, with a panoramic view of the old town. It has an excellent restaurant (tel: 7252-53410).

There are many modest cafés

*Mahler found Maria Wörth an inspiring summer home*

and restaurants, including several on the Stadtplatz. At **Torggelen Weistube** you can enjoy good local food.

### Tourist Office

Fremdenverkehrsverband Steyr, Stadtplatz 27, A-4400 (tel: 7252-53229).

### Excursions

In summer there are trips to the countryside on a narrow-gauge railway with steam engines. Seventeen miles (28km) to the west of Steyr, is the little town of **Kremsmünster**, dominated by a massive Benedictine abbey. This has undergone the usual Gothic and baroque remodelling; highlights are a fine library, superb decoration in the Kaisersaal (imperial apartments), and an 8th-century chalice in the Abteitrakt (Treasury). In the observatory, an eight-storey tower, there's a science museum.

About 11 miles (17km) to the east of Steyr is another Benedictine abbey – at **Seitenstetten**. Only the medieval Ritterkapelle (Knights' Chapel) survives, with an excellent collection of paintings.

## ◆◆
## WÖRTHER SEE
*Kärnten*

The Riviera of central Europe, the Wörther See has long been a favoured holiday resort of Austria's celebrities, past and present (Mahler had a home here). The lake, 10½ miles (17km) long, is so warm that you can swim here from early May; inevitably, it is crowded in summer.

Surrounded by woods and particularly fine scenery, the whole seems specially designed, like a stage set. The decision facing visitors is whether to pay star prices at the fashionable resorts, or opt for a cheaper and quieter stay somewhere near by, perhaps on one of the other lakes in the region.

Boat trips are the best way to see the lake. There are lots of possibilities – round trips, old steamers, cruises, some accompanied by bands. Sports facilities around the lake are superb, and include cycle tracks and several golf courses. The two main resorts on the Wörther See are Pörtschach and Velden. **Velden**, at the west end of the lake, is the beautiful people's resort, with prices to match: classy, chic, and good fun in August, when there is a carnival. **Pörtschach**, on the north shore, is a fair size resort on a peninsula, with busy day and nightlife, and fine promenades for evening strolls. Three miles (5km) to the east, **Krumpendorf** is an immaculate spa village with lots of public gardens.

The main sight on the lake is **Maria Wörth**, a wonderfully picturesque village set on a rocky promontory, with two pilgrimage churches, all of which have been the subject of a million photographs.

### Accommodation

There are many good four- and five-star hotels around the lake, in varying styles of architecture. Most offer a good choice of sports facilities. **Parkhotel Pörtschach**, Elisabethstrasse 22 (tel: 4272-26210) is large and modern, while **Hotel Schloss Leonstain**, Hauptstrasse 228 (tel: 4272-28160) is more homely.

Velden boasts the **Seehotel Hubertushof**, Europaplatz 1, A-9220 (tel: 4274-2655), a turn-of-the-century family-run complex comprising two resort houses in original art-deco style, situated directly on the lake.

There are plenty of places to stay in Maria Wörth.

The four-star **Wörth** (tel: 4273-2276) lies above the lake; the **Strandhotel Sille**, Wörtherseestrasse 36 (tel: 4273-2237, is on the lakeside. Flats and bungalows are available too, some in beautiful locations. **Seehaus Ing Brigitte Stapf** has its own boathouse and is set amid weeping willows by the waterside.

### Tourist Office

Fremdenverkehrsamt A-9081 Maria Wörth Wörthersee-Süd (tel: 4273-22400).

### Other Lakes in
### South Carinthia

Just to the east of Villach lies the little **Faaker See**, in a gorgeous setting bordered by the

## THE CENTRE

Karawanken mountain range to the south, and the Villach Alps to the west. This lake is one of the quietest and prettiest in the region.

To the east is the **Keutschacher See**, similar to Faaker, and also set in fine scenery. This is ideal walking and camping country. Northwest of Villach is the **Millstätter See**, another beauty, rimmed by woods and snowy peaks. At **Millstatt** itself there is a former Benedictine abbey, and a continuous music festival, lasting from spring to autumn. Just to the northeast of Villach is the **Ossiacher See**, yet another pretty lake. The small town of Ossiach stages the Carinthian Summer Festival in July and August, and gets very busy.

---

### Carinthian Churches and Castles

**Friesach** (*26 miles* (*41km*) *north of Klagenfurt*) This fortress town on the old trade route between Vienna and Venice is a good base for castle and church visiting. Medieval town walls, towers and moat have survived, and there are interesting churches and houses in the centre. In the Dominican monastery, plays and concerts are staged in summer.

**Gurk** (*31 miles* (*49km*) *north of Klagenfurt*) This little town and pilgrimage centre has one of the most important Romanesque churches in the country. A site of worship since the Celts, Gurk was built between 1140 and 1200. The basilica has two baroque onion domes, fine Gothic frescos in the porch, and wonderful Romanesque murals in the Bishop's Chapel. Impressive too are the gilt high altar, baroque pulpit and the crypt, full of white marble columns.

**Hochosterwitz** (*14 miles* (*23km*) *northeast of Klagenfurt*) This extraordinary fortress glowers down from an outcrop of limestone high above the valley. Built between 1570 and 1586, it served as a Protestant haven and sheltered the local populace (and their animals). The long approach ramp has 14 defensive gates.

**Maria Saal** (*6 miles* (*10km*) *north of Klagenfurt*) Pilgrimage centre, and one of the region's finest churches, Maria Saal has survived a Hungarian siege and was one of the first bastions of Christianity. On a Roman site, the double-towered Gothic church underwent Renaissance and baroque refits. The vaulted and painted interior is harmonious. More notable perhaps is the octagonal charnel house.

**Schloss Porcia** (*At Spittal an der Drau, 22 miles* (*35km*) *northwest of Villach*) A fine Renaissance palace, with an arcaded courtyard, housing a regional museum.

**St Paul im Lavanttal** (*34 miles* (*54km*) *northeast of Klagenfurt*) Perched above an attractive village, surrounded by orchards and vineyards, this Benedictine abbey possesses one of the finest Romanesque churches in the area. There are twin towers, finely carved capitals and 15th-century frescos. The abbey also has a rich art collection and library.

## THE WEST

Mother Earth has been kind to Western Austria, endowing it with an improbable beauty usually found only in picture books. The landscape of majestic mountains, dazzling lakes and wild gorges is complemented by the villages, colourful with carved and painted chalets hung with flowers; all around are meadows tinkling with the sound of cow bells. This is also the land of ski resorts, which easily convert to summer activities, and of the mighty Grossglockner, Austria's highest peak and gateway to the sublime Hohe Tauern National Park. And in the centre, amid a wonderful array of mountains of course, lies Innsbruck, the capital of the Tirol, another architectural treasure trove.

This section covers the provinces of Vorarlberg and Tirol, the separate area of Ost Tirol (East Tirol), and the western parts of Land Salzburg and Kärnten (Carinthia). Vorarlberg is a province apart, close in both geographical and cultural respects to Switzerland, with which it shares a common dialect. After the fall of the Habsburgs, it elected to join Switzerland, but was rejected. The province is often bypassed by visitors, but its valleys and mountains are equal to any, and its capital, Bregenz, has an international reputation for opera.

*Heiligenblut below Grossglockner*

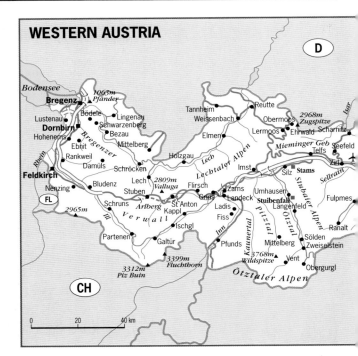

**WESTERN AUSTRIA**

The Tirol, by contrast, is a showpiece province geared towards tourism, yet managing to retain its rural Alpine charm. A mecca for sports enthusiasts throughout the year, the area exudes wealth and health. The Tirol people are friendly and fiercely independent; their hero (apart from Olympic skiers) is Andreas Hofer, the freedom fighter who saved the Tirol three times before it finally fell to Napoleon. The loss of South Tirol to Italy following World War I is still a sore subject. The little sister province of Ost (East) Tirol is separated from the rest of the Tirol by Land Salzburg.

## WHAT TO SEE

### ◆◆
### ARLBERG
The Arlberg massif marks the watershed between the Danube and the Rhine, and divorces the people of the Vorarlberg from their eastern neighbours – a parting as much cultural as physical. In 1978 an 8½-mile (14km) road tunnel was finished under the desolate Arlberg Pass 5,882 feet (1,793m).
**St Anton-am-Arlberg** is the largest resort of the area, frequented in winter by royalty and celebrities. and famous for its contribution to the history of modern skiing. Now bypassed

by the Arlberg tunnel road, the long narrow resort centre is not as pretty as many others; but it is a lively place, and there are plenty of sports facilities (including mountain bike runs) and an excellent network of mountain lifts which offer access to the upper reaches of the Valluga, Gampen and Kapall peaks.

A music festival in August is followed by the September 'Eagles Meeting', when a series of specially designed hikes is arranged.

The other main resort of the

*Walking in the mountains. Health addicts will find this hard to beat*

region is **Lech**, beautifully set on a river, in a bowl of grassy slopes. It too is well provided with sports facilities of all kinds, including angling; and organised events include lantern-lit walks, and mountain hut parties. Children are particularly well catered for, and special adventure programmes arranged.

The route between Lech and St Anton leads over the beautiful **Flexen Pass**. Six miles (10km) west of St Anton, **Stuben** is a small, tranquil and relatively unspoilt village, which used to serve as a resting place for climbers about to embark on the Arlberg Pass.

### Accommodation

In St Anton, the four-star **Alte Post** (tel: 5446-25530) and the **Schwarzer Adler** (tel: 5446-22440) are both central, and in beautiful old buildings. On a more modest level is the **Gasthof Pension Friedheim** (tel: 5446-2411).

Lech has a large number of very comfortable hotels. The most luxurious and stylish are the beautiful and traditional **Post** (tel: 5583-22060) and the modern **Arlberg** (tel: 5583-2134). The four-star **Tannbergerhof** (tel: 5583-2202) is lively. The two-star **Bergblick** and **Gasthof Auerhahn** have plenty of atmosphere.

### Tourist Offices

Fremdenverkehrsbüro, St Anton-am-Arlberg, A-6580 tel: 5446-22690).

Fremdenverkehrsbüro, Lech-am-Arlberg, A-6764 (tel: 5583-216126).

◆◆
## BREGENZ
*Vorarlberg*

At the eastern end of the Bodensee (Lake Constance), Bregenz is the capital of the Vorarlberg. This small pleasant town, beautifully fringed by lake and mountains, has a good track record in staging festivals, and becomes a lively place to stay in summer.

Bregenz falls into two parts. The higher old town, which still has evidence of fortified walls, and the lower lakeshore area, 'Unter', which was covered by the lake in the early Middle Ages.

Along the shore to the west are gardens, sports complexes and a huge bathing area with several pools. Centrally sited is the **Festspiel und Kongresshaus**, home of the superb summer festival (July/August). Its famous floating stage, on a rocky pier jutting into the lake, can be seen by over 4,000 spectators. The design is such that both open-air and closed concerts can be enjoyed. Away from the shore to the east is **Kornmarktplatz** with the Theatre in a grain warehouse, and the **Landesmuseum** (Provincial Museum) with prehistoric exhibits, arts and crafts, tapestries and paintings – including those of Angelika Kaufmann (see **Bregenzerwald**). Just behind is the rococo **Nepomukkapelle**, now the Hungarian Church. On Kornmarktstrasse is the baroque inn, the **Gasthof Kornmesser**. The quieter old town has cobbled streets and half-

*A lovely lakeside town, Zell am See was visited by D H Lawrence*

timbered houses. Past the 16th-century gate is the onion-domed **Martinsturm**; at its foot is a chapel with notable 14th-century frescos. A short walk across the Thalbach ravine leads to **Pfarrkirche St Gallus** (parish church), a Gothic building with baroque additions and fine carvings.

For a fine view of the lake, you can take a cable car (or walk) up to the **Pfänder** peak; at the top, (3,491 feet/1,064m) is a restaurant.

## Tourist Office

Fremdenverkehrsamt, Anton Schneider Strasse 4a, A-6900 Bregenz (tel: 5574-433910).

## Excursions

The forests, peaks and rich valleys of the **Bregenzerwald** form a picturesque semi-circle to the southeast of the town, and offer ideal walking or hiking country.

The villagers here often dress in bright, colourful local costumes; and some of the houses are decorated with wood shingle. Resorts include **Bezau**, **Damüls** (the highest village in the area), **Lingenau**, **Schröcken**, the last village before the Hochtannberg Pass, (5,508 feet/1,679m), and **Schwarzenberg**, probably the most picturesque and colourful village of all. This was the home of the painter Angelika Kaufmann (1741–1807), who spent much time in England;

her work can be seen in the church. A delightful hotel in Schwarzenberg is **Gasthof Adler** (tel: 5512-2966), which is set in a fine traditional building.

**Dornbirn**, 8 miles (13km) south of Bregenz, is the commercial centre of the Bregenzerwald, with a flourishing textile industry.

From here, a road and then a track lead along the spectacular **Rappenlochschlucht** (Rappenloch Gorge) to Ebnit. At the **Alplochschlucht** ravine, there is a high waterfall.

Four miles (6km) southwest of Dornbirn, at **Hohenems**, a Schubertiade festival is held in the 16th-century *Schloss* annually in June. In the 18th century, parts of the Nibelungenlied manuscript were found here; they were to form the basis for Wagner's Ring Cycle opera.

The **Bodele**, about 9 miles (14km) southeast of Bregenz, is a perfect summer spot, with lakes, fields and forests, and views across the Bodensee.

**Feldkirch**, 22 miles (35km) southwest of Bregenz, close to the principality of Liechtenstein, is a pretty market town with cobbled streets and arcaded houses, surrounded by steep cliffs on the north banks of the Ill. The old town has kept its medieval layout, and the 15th-century 'Cat's Tower', with its huge bell, attests to its key position on the main route through the Arlberg. Local events include a Schubertiade Lieder festival in June, a wine festival in July, and a gathering of jugglers in August.

◆◆◆
## GROSSGLOCKNER HOCHALPENSTRASSE ✓

*Salzburg and Kärnten*

To see the mountains at their most majestic, the 30 miles (48km) of Grossglockner mountain road cannot be equalled. Built in 1935, the toll road starts at Bruck, just south of Zell am See, following a wooded gorge. Hairpin bends mark the climb from Ferleiten to Fuscher Törl amid 10,000-foot (3,000-m) peaks. Like a cinemascope film, each turn offers a more stupendous vista.

On the way to the top of the pass, the summit of the Edelweissspitze has an observation tower. The northern entrance to the Hochtor Tunnel marks the highest point, (8,218 feet/2,505m); staggering views await travellers at the southern exit.

From the Guttal ravine, a 'Glacier Route' leads in a series of twisting turns to Franz-Josef's Höhe, home of a mountaineering school, where a viewing terrace surveys the magnificent Pasterze Glacier (reached by a funicular). The road gets crowded in summer, resulting in tail-backs to the observation points.

At the bottom of the Grossglockner's southern slope, little **Heiligenblut** may come as a welcome relief after the relentless parade of nature's wonders. Here the sight of interest is man-made: the Gothic Pfarrkirche (parish church) and pilgrimage centre, with a slender steeple, and a superb painted winged altar.

The southern section of road leads over the **Iselsbergpass**, (3,950 feet/1,204m), from where there are fine views towards the toothy crags of the Dolomites south of the pleasant little town of **Lienz** which lies at the junction of several valleys. (Also see **Peace and Quiet**, page 92).

### ◆◆◆
### INNSBRUCK ✓

*Tirol*

The Tirol finds a synthesis in its capital city Innsbruck. Although the iridescent curtain of mountains seems to surge to its

*Maria-Theresien Strasse, Innsbruck*

## THE WEST

very doorstep, the city owes much of its growth to its position at the crossroads of European trade routes. Now it seamlessly knits its Alpine traditions with commerce – notably tourism and sport.

At the junction of the River Inn and the Sill gap, Innsbruck is girdled by the Karwendel massif to the north, and the Stubai and Tuxer Alps in the south. The city centre is another Austrian baroque beauty, little changed for centuries. The cathedral and university add to its dignity, but the physical vitality comes from the mountains. Two Winter Olympics (in 1964 and 1976) have resulted in superb facilities, including a famous ski jump that towers over the city and gives jumpers the uncanny impression that they are heading for a cemetery which backs on to it.

### History

Innsbruck has changed hands several times. From Celtic and Roman origins, it grew into a market settlement and then a town, coming under Habsburg control from the 14th to the 17th centuries. Emperor Maximilian I (1490–1519) and Empress Maria Theresia (1717–80) made important contributions to the development of its art and culture.

Napoleon ceded Innsbruck and the Tirol to Bavaria in 1806; liberation struggles led by Andreas Hofer were only temporarily successful and the Tirol was back in Bavarian control by 1809. Austria won it back after the Congress of Vienna (1815) and Innsbruck became the capital of the Tirol. The opening up of the south, in the form of the 19th-century

*Innsbruck's picturesque setting*

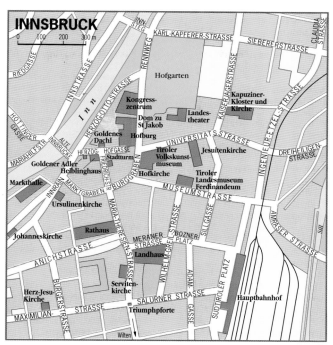

Brenner Railway, marked a renewal in Innsbruck's growth. Now it acts as host to international trade fairs.

### Sightseeing

In Innsbruck's Altstadt (Old Town), imperial history accounts for a wealth of lavishly decorated public buildings, Renaissance and baroque. Fine examples of Tirolean architecture can be found: beautiful town houses with arcaded fronts and oriel windows.

Part of the Old Town is pedestrianised, within the streets known as Graben (moat). Here, **Herzog-Friedrich Strasse** has many superb houses with Gothic and Renaissance features; the jewel in the crown is the Rennaisance **Goldenes Dachl** (Golden Roof). This gilded-tile loggia was built in the 1490s to celebrate Maximilian's marriage; it served as a royal viewing gallery for watching festivities in the square below, and symbolised the dynasty's power. When the sun shines, it is an amazing sight; unfortunately, the rest of the building, which was altered in 1822, seems rather dull by comparison.

The Golden Roof now houses an Olympic museum.

Opposite, the late Gothic **Heiblinghaus** also catches the eye: the multi-coloured rococo remodel has much ornate stucco detail, with cherubs fighting for space with leaves, flowers and scrolls. Near by is the 16th-century **Goldener Adler** (Golden Eagle) and the 15th-century **Stadtturm** (Watch Tower).

To the north is the **Dom zu St Jakob** (St Jacob's Cathedral), built in 1722, with a lavish interior even by baroque standards. Above the altar hangs Lucas Cranach's Mariahilf, and an intricately carved pulpit also stands out. In Hofgasse is the **Hofburg** (Imperial Palace), a composite structure built for various Habsburg archdukes; Maria Theresia is responsible for the present one. Luxurious rococo apartments abound, including the Riesensaal (Giants' Hall) layered with white and gold porcelain stucco decoration and frescos by Maulbertsch, the distinguished master of baroque painting.

Near by is the **Hofkirche** (Court Church), containing a stunning Renaissance black marble tomb, elaborately surrounded by statues detailing the life and times of Maximilian I, for whom the church was intended as a mausoleum. Another people's hero, freedom fighter Andreas Hofer, is interred here. In the Silberne Kapelle (Silver Chapel), so called because of the silver Madonna on the altar, lies the tomb of Archduke Ferdinand II.

Situated next to the Hofkirche is the splendid **Tiroler Volkskunstmuseum** (Tirolean Folk Art Museum), a highly regarded collection of local arts and crafts. To the south, in Museumstrasse, is the **Tiroler Landesmuseum Ferdinandeum**, a provincial museum which has a good collection of Tirolean art, especially from the Gothic period.

Maria-Theresien Strasse is the city's main shopping street, lined with fine shops, cafés, and 17th- and 18th-century houses. It presents a striking picture, with a **Triumphpforte** (Triumphal Arch) built to mark both the marriage of the would-be Leopold II and the death of Franz I; the baroque masterpiece of the **Landhaus** building; and a backdrop of 7,545-foot (2,300-m) high mountains.

To the south of the centre of Innsbruck, the district of Wilten possesses in its **Pfarrkirche** one of the loveliest rococo churches in the area, well worth a visit. Opposite is the **Stift Wilten** (Wilten Abbey), built by the Premonstratensian Order. A giant Gothic stone statue stands in the church porch. Near by lies **Bergisel**, the ski jump hill, also famous as the site where bitter battles were fought for the Tirol's freedom in 1809.

## Entertainment and Sport

Innsbruck is a great place in which to have fun. Something is going on throughout the year, but in August a big festival of early music is staged. Many concerts (especially organ) take place in churches, palaces and museums. The city also has its own symphony orchestra,

and lots of brass folk bands.
There are plays and dancing at
the Landestheater, concerts and
exhibitions in the Hofgarten
(Palace Gardens), plus lots of
jazz.
Innsbruck is a major centre for
sport. South of Wilten, the
Bergisel hill has lots of facilities,
apart from the ski jump –
including archery, bowling,
cycling, golf and rafting. Club
Innsbruck grants automatic
membership to anyone staying
longer than three days,
enabling visitors to join in a
hiking programme or get
reductions on sports, museums,
and the Alpen Zoo (see below).
There are two climbing schools,
and summer skiing is possible
on the Stubai glacier.

## Accommodation
The central four-star **Goldener
Adler**, Herzog-Friedrich
Strasse 6 (tel: 512-586334), has
played host to royalty and
celebrities; it has a wine bar,
and notable restaurant. The
four-star **Alpotel**, Innrain 13
(tel: 512-577931) is more
modern, but has an elegant
restaurant. The attractive three-

*Take a break and enjoy open-air
dining in the Old City, Innsbruck*

star **Weisses Kreuz**, Herzog-
Friedrich Strasse, is more
modestly priced (tel: 512-
59479). There are plenty of
guesthouses, such as the three-
star **Bierwirt**, Bichlweg 2 (tel:
512-342143), the two-star **Engl**,
Innstrasse 22 (tel: 512-294258),
or the two-star **Laurin**,
Gumppstrasse 19 (tel: 512-
341104).

## Tourist Office
Verkehrsbüro, Burggraben 3,
A-6021 Innsbruck (tel: 512-
5356). Information on the Tirol
is available from Bozner Platz 7,
A-6021 Innsbruck (tel: 512-
59850).

## Excursions
On the north bank of the Inn,
about 1½ miles (3km) from the
centre, the **Alpen Zoo** is a high-
altitude zoo where animals are
kept in their natural
environment; it is reached by
funicular up the **Hungerburg**,
(2,739 feet/835m). A trip here
could also include a two-stage
cable car trip, from the top of
Hungerburg to **Seegrube**,

(6,247 feet/1,904m) and
**Hafelekar**, (7,500 feet/2,286m);
views are memorable, and
there are restaurants en route.
Two miles (4km) southeast of
the city is the former home of
Archduke Ferdinand II (1563–
95), **Schloss Ambras**, one of the
most attractive and best-
preserved castles in the
country. It houses a museum
with fine collections, in
particular of portraits and
armour; its splendid Spanish
Hall is a venue for concerts.
A point of interest 6 miles
(10km) along the route south
from Innsbruck to Italy via the
Brenner Pass is the impressive
**Europabrücke** (bridge) which
spans the Sill: it measures 2,690
feet (820m), and is 623 feet
(190m) high.
Twenty-one miles (34km) to the
west of Innsbruck lies the
Cistercian abbey of **Stams**. The
original abbey buildings were
much damaged – the current
building dates from the 17th

century, and the church is
mainly baroque in style. The
high altar, which is in the shape
of a Tree of Life, is a memorable
sight.
On a broad plateau above the
Inn valley, 13 miles (21km)
northwest of Innsbruck, the
well-established and well-
ordered resort of **Seefeld** could
serve as a relaxing base from
which to make excursions to,
rather than from, Innsbruck. It is
neat, comfortable, and well
endowed with sports facilities
(there is an excellent new
sports centre); lake activities,
concerts of traditional music,
horse-and-carriage rides and a
casino are just some of the other
options.

◆◆
## KITZBÜHEL
*Tirol*
One of Austria's oldest and most
famous ski resorts, Kitzbühel is
well liked in summer too. Set in
a pretty, wooded valley, the
town gained its wealth in the
16th and 17th centuries through

*Mountain scenery at Kitzbühel*

copper and silver mining. The old gabled houses are still intact and brightly painted, creating a festive atmosphere; there are two interesting churches.

Mountains cast shadows over the town: the Kitzbüheler Horn (6,562 feet/2,000m) and the Hahnenkamm, (5,430 feet/1,655m), the site of one of the world's most famous downhill ski races. Near the top of the **Kitzbüheler Horn** (a five-hour climb, or toll road or cable car), a large Alpine garden has been landscaped.

Near to the northeast of town is the **Schwarzsee**, suitable for bathing. Also just outside is the **Hinterobenau Farmhouse Museum**.

### Accommodation

There are many large and comfortable top-class hotels in town, including the central **Tennerhof** (tel: 5356-3181) or the **Weisses Rössl** (tel: 5356-2541). A modest and much cheaper alternative is the quiet and central **Pension Maria Hilde** (tel: 5356-3130).

### Tourist Office

Kitzbühel Tourismus A-6370, Kitzbühel (tel: 5356-2155).

### Excursions

The rugged massif of the **Kaisergebirge** (16 miles (25km) northwest of Kitzbühel) can be reached via the busy town of St Johann in Tirol and a small road from Griesenau which penetrates the heart of the mountains. To the southwest of the massif is the lovely **Hintersteinersee**, reached from Scheffau.

### ÖTZTALER ALPEN

*Tirol*

Three main valleys lead to the river Inn from the Ötztaler Alps: the Ötztal, the Pitztal, and the Kaunertal. The largest, and best known, is the **Ötztal**, the valley of the Ötztaler Ache (river). Twisting paths, waterfalls, gorges and expanses of meadow line the extremely beautiful route along the river, above which tower massive peaks and glaciers.

**Umhausen** is a pretty resort and base for climbers; an hour's walk away are the dramatic **Stuiben waterfall**. **Längenfeld**, a spa village, can cater for more visitors, and has little mountain huts for the ultimate get-away-from-it-all break.

**Sölden** and **Höchsölden** are the centre of the upper Ötztal holiday region, offering summer skiing and cable cars to panoramic views. Southwest from Zwieselstein, a steep mountain road (1 in 3.5 gradient) leads to the picturesque **Vent** villages, dominated magnificently by the highest point in the north Tirol, the **Wildspitze**. At the end of the road, **Rofenhöhe** is the highest occupied all-year village in Austria, (6,608 feet/2,014m), in a cradle of mountains which all tower above (9,840 feet/3,000m). Just to the east, in **Gurgltal**, lies the ski resort of **Obergurgl**, Austria's highest parish, with an Alpine climbing school for experienced climbers. Beyond is a spectacular toll route, the **Hochalpenstrasse** into Italy (open June to October only).

To the west of Ötztal, the sunny **Pitztal** is ideal for a quiet holiday, once again amid glorious scenery, with good climbs and summer skiing. **Mittelberg**, at the head of the valley, is especially delightful. The road along the **Kaunertal**, further west, is scenic but demanding, through decorative villages past the **Gepatsch** reservoir. From there the road becomes a panoramic glacier route rising to over 8,990 feet (2,740m). Beyond this, a chair lift plus a 20-minute climb leads to a stunning view over Austria, Italy and Switzerland.

The Ötztaler Alpen themselves are a paradise for climbers, and many of the highest peaks (apart from the rugged Kauner Grat between Pitztal and Kaunertal) are not especially difficult.

### Tourist Office
Fremdenverkehrsverband Innerötztal, A-6450 Sölden, Tirol (tel: 5254-221221).

### ZELL AM SEE
*Salzburg*

The attractive old lakeside town of Zell am See promotes itself as the centre of one of Austria's principal sporting areas – the 'Europa Sport Region' – and aims to provide an even better range of sporting facilities than other resorts. Although many of the sports available are for the ultra-keen, or the aspiring mountaineer, Zell can also provide more gentle alternatives, such as riding and boat trips; the resort also has an attractive pedestrianised old town area, lake promenades, and a good network of lifts for mountain excursions.

### Accommodation
Among the nicest of the simple three-star flower-decked chalet hotels in Zell are the **Pension Gruber**, Dorfplatz 9 (tel: 6542-3181) and the **Pension Alpenheim**, Salzachtal Bundesstrasse 34 (tel: 6542-77234). In the heart of the old town is the attractive four-star **Fischerwirt** (tel: 6542-2675); the large lakeside **Grand Hotel Mövenpick** (tel: 6542-2388) has several restaurants, and its own stretch of bathing beach.

### Tourist Office
Fremdenverkehrsbüro Zell am See, A-5700 (tel: 6542-2600).

### Excursions
Just to the southwest, the **Kaprunertal** (another sports centre) is known for summer skiing, and offers lots of excursions – in particular to two large reservoirs in high mountain settings.

North of Zell am See, the stretch of the **Saalach** valley north of Saalfelden edges the steep rock wall of the **Steinernes Meer** (Sea of Stone). At the **Seisenbergklamm** (19 miles/30km north of Zell), you can walk along the roaring **Weissbach** torrent (allow about an hour); and just a little further there are illuminated caves at **Lamprechtshöhle**.

### ZILLERTAL
*Tirol, Salzburg*

The Ziller River runs north to join the Inn from the Zillertal Alpen which border Italy, and where it is joined by several

## Go For It!

Western Austria's mountains and lakes are Europe's ultimate adventure playground, whether you are seven or 70. Here is the chance to get the buzz of taking risks, learn a new sport, know the thrill of achievement, and have the best guides and tuition possible.

Even the smallest resorts can offer swimming pools and tennis courts; larger ones may have golf courses. Most run children's programmes. The list below is a taster of the more off-beat sports available, and just a few places where you can try them; it is well worth asking at tourist offices what is available locally. Major centres are the Ötztal, Mayrhofen in the Zillertal, St Anton, and the 'Europa Sport Region', which includes Zell am See and Kaprun near the Grossglockner. This area offers a different adventure sport (including crevasse rescue techniques) every day in a special 'Mount Alpin' package.

- **Summer tobogganing** Saalfelden (near Zell am See); St Johann in Tirol
- **Summer glacier skiing** Hintertux (Zillertal); Kaprun; Kaunertal and Pitztal; Sölden
- **Mountaineering and rock climbing** Ötztal; Kaprun; Mayrhofen (includes a school for beginners)
- **'Hiking Light'** (your luggage is taken on ahead to the next stop, while you walk) Saalfelden (near Zell am See); Vorarlberg (information from Bregenz)
- **Trekking** Karwendel Massif (two-day tour) Stubai Massif (high trail for the fit)
- **Sailing** Bregenz
- **River rafting** Mayrhofen
- **Gold panning** Heiligenblut
- **Mountain biking** St Anton
- **Pony trekking** Grossglockner region
- **Paragliding and hang-gliding** Ötztal area; Kössen, near German border north of Kitzbühel (international competitions).

Other activities include hot air ballooning, cycling, archery, and children's adventure programmes.

smaller rivers; here, high up in the mountains, little blue lakes reflect the icy crests, and contribute their charm to some delightful walks.

In the north, the Zillertal is a busy and wooded valley. Its main centre is the market town of **Zell am Ziller** which bustles in early May with the Gauderfest.

**Mayrhofen** is a major resort,

*Hotel Neuhaus, Mayrhofen*

# THE WEST

lively and friendly, with excellent facilities – including a large new sports complex. The Sport Hotel Strass's subterranean 'Arena' club is an unexpectedly sophisticated venue for concerts of popular music.

South of Mayrhofen the scenery is spectacular, and small roads offer opportunities to visit old Tirolean villages – such as **Brandberg** (3 miles/5km east of Mayrhofen), much loved by artists.

To the west of Mayrhofen, the **Tuxertal** road leads to a summer glacier skiing region (at over 9,840 feet/3,000m). **Lanersbach** is a pretty village, **Hintertux** a small ski resort and spa set at the foot of steep mountains.

## Accommodation
Mayrhofen has a good range of traditionally styled hotels and bed-and-breakfast places. The new and very attractive five-star **Elisabeth**, just off Mayrhofen's main street (tel: 5285-2929), has its own pool. The refurbished 17th-century four-star **Kramerwirt** (tel: 5285-2615) is also in the centre, and has lots of charm.

## Tourist Office
Tourismusverband Mayrhofen, Dursterstrasse 225, Postfach 21, A-6290 Mayrhofen (tel: 5285-2305).

## Excursions
Just north of Jenbach, on the Inn, the large lake of **Achensee** may serve as a change from mountains and meadows. The lake villages of Pertisau and Maurach are very pretty.

In the neighbouring valley, northeast of the Zillertal, **Alpbach** is an idyllic picture-book village, with old wooden chalets, flower-strewn pastures, and a background of pine woods.

The road along the narrow, wooded **Gerlostal**, an eastern tributary of the Ziller, winds over the **Gerlospass** (5,348 feet/1,630m; toll payable) and leads down to the massive **Krimml waterfalls**, a very popular excursion from Innsbruck and even Salzburg. To see all the falls, including the 'upper' ones, you should allow about four hours.

## ◆◆
## ZUGSPITZE
*Tirol*
The mighty peak of the Zugspitze, 9,716 feet (2,963m) lies on the border with Germany. A cable car goes from Obermoos to Zugspitzkamm station, at 9,203 feet (2,805m), from where there are superb views over the pine woods of the Loisach valley, and the Lechtal Alps. A second cable car goes to the summit, where the views take in the Grossglockner glacier, the Stubai and Ziller Alps, the Bernina range and the Arlberg. To the north are the Bavarian lowlands and lakes. As this is cross-border territory, you will need to take your passport. **Ehrwald**, on the access route, is a pretty village and a good base for exploring and hiking. Just to the west, the village of **Lermoos** is larger but marginally less attractive. To the south is the lakeland area of the **Fernpass**.

# *Peace and Quiet*

*Wildlife and Countryside in Austria by Paul Sterry*

Everything, from wetlands and huge lakes to forests and Alpine peaks, makes Austria an unexpectedly varied country. It has immense scope for hiking and relaxation, with an abundance of wildlife to match the often stunning scenery. Within the borders of Austria, birdwatchers can expect to find almost all the species that central Europe has to offer. But the eastern part of the country, and Burgenland in particular, offers surprises. There, remnant pockets of the once great Hungarian Plain extend over the Austrian border and harbour many unusual species. The presence of the huge lake called Neusiedler See makes this region one of the most exciting and varied for wildlife in the whole of the country.

**Neusiedler See**
Twenty-two miles (35km) long and up to 9 miles (15km) wide, this huge lake lies on the Hungarian border southeast of Vienna. It is shallow – nowhere much deeper than 6 feet (2m) – and fringed by vast reedbeds and marshlands. Large numbers and an extraordinary range of birds breed here,

*Little egret*

including herons, egrets, warblers and wildfowl. In short, it is one of *the* birdwatching locations in central Europe. Neusiedler See can be viewed from many points around its margin. There are minor roads giving access to the shores of the lake or to the reedbeds at

## PEACE AND QUIET

### White Stork

Visitors to the Neusiedler
See area should have little
difficulty in seeing white
storks. These huge birds –
mainly white but with black
wing feathers and red bill
and feet – are summer
visitors and are often seen
feeding in fields and
meadows. However, they
are most often noticed in the
villages, such as Rust and
Illmitz, that border the lake.
In these settings, the large
untidy nests of twigs and
branches are difficult to
miss, perched as they are on
roof tops.

Local people believe that to
have a stork nesting on a
house confers good luck on
its residents, so many
villagers put old cart wheels
on their roofs to encourage
the birds to come to nest.

Rust, Neusiedl-am-See,
Podersdorf and Illmitz. For
naturalists, the track from Illmitz
to the shore of the lake is
probably the best. Stop and
look at Zick Lacke en route for
waders and herons and, where
the road passes through the
reedbeds, for warblers and
penduline tits. The latter are
endearing little birds that build
bottle-shaped nests suspended
from the branches of wetland
shrubs and bushes.

Close to the edge of the eastern
shores of Neusiedler See is the
Oberstinkersee, a much
smaller lake also rich in bird
life. A road runs along part of its
eastern margin. Halfway along
the road from Podersdorf south
to Illmitz, a track heads west
towards Neusiedler See. It runs

around the shores of the
Oberstinkersee – use your car
as a 'mobile hide' and look for
birds such as avocets, ruff and
white-winged black terns. Just
to the south is the
Unterstinkersee, which is also
good for birds.

### Lange Lacke

The flat terrain east of Neusiedler
See, known as the Seewinkel, is
studded with shallow, alkaline
lakes (called *Lacken*), three of
which have already been
mentioned. Lange Lacke is a
particularly large body of water
and is protected by nature
reserve status. There is a car
park beside the road between
Apetlon and Wallern im
Burgenland, and a signboard
describes the layout of the
reserve and the tracks to follow.
The meadows that surround it
are full of colourful flowers in

### Great Bustard

The great bustard is
Europe's heaviest bird, and
one of the largest birds
capable of sustained flight.
Males are larger than
females and when mature
have elegant plumes on the
neck and wings which are
used in displays to impress
the females.

Despite their size, bustards
are wary birds and have been
much persecuted by man
over the centuries. Loss of
habitat is a factor that has also
contributed to their decline.
They like wide open spaces of
grassland, and changes in
land use and disturbance
caused by agriculture do not
favour them.

spring and summer, with the deep blue of spiked speedwell among the most attractive. Field crickets and wartbiter bush crickets live in the meadows; these are spectacular insects that may be present in large numbers during the summer months. Waders and terns can be abundant on the lake, especially during migration periods in spring and autumn.

**Tadten Plain**
The Tadten Plain is a flat area of land, once rich in colourful flowers and grassland wildlife, which is continuous with the Hansag or Hungarian Plain across the Hungarian border. Minor roads cross the area southeast of the road between Wallern im Burgenland and Tadten – explore using your car as a mobile hide. Most of the area has been turned into agricultural land, but a small area directly southeast from Tadten village has been preserved for its flora and fauna, and in particular for its great bustards. Look for an elevated viewing platform beside the road and a *Naturschutzgebiet* signpost for Trappe Hansag (*Grosse Trappe* is the Austrian name for great bustard). View the bustards from the platform and *do not* attempt to enter the reserve itself.

**Hohe Wand**
This high rocky outcrop – part of the Wiener Hausberge – lies south of Vienna, west of Wiener Neustadt. Rising from a landscape of rolling farmland, Hohe Wand is dramatic and imposing enough from its base. From the top of the plateau, however, the views are even more spectacular, stretching for miles on a clear day.
Hohe Wand is signposted and easily visible from route 222. There is parking at the foot of the cliff face as well as at the top in several places. There is also

*Great bustards can be seen in their protected habitat at Tadten*

# PEACE AND QUIET

an interpretive centre on the plateau.

At the foot of the cliff are areas of rich meadows which are full of colourful flowers and butterflies. Patches of woodland harbour interesting birds such as nutcrackers and woodpeckers, and a few trees cling precariously to rocky outcrops and ledges on the cliff itself.

A narrow road winds its way tortuously up the face of the cliff and eventually levels out on the top of the plateau. You can park in several places and walk to the cliff edge to admire the view. Take great care when you are near the edge – the drop is precipitous.

Many of the plants and animals that live on the top of Hohe Wand are true Alpine species. If you sit carefully near the cliff edge, you can watch the rocks below for chamois. These nimble-footed creatures are entirely confident on even the

*Alpine chough*

narrowest of ledges and seemingly oblivious to the horrifying drop below them. Birds of prey glide by on the updraughts off the cliff face, sometimes flying on eye-level with observers on top of the plateau.

## Marchauen

This pristine area of riverine forest lies on the Slovakian border between the towns of Marchegg and Baumgarten. It can easily be reached on a day trip from Vienna. Take the road which runs northeast from Vienna to Angern close to the border, and head south to Marchegg on the road which runs parallel with the border. The reserve entrance is on the outskirts of the village of Marchegg and is marked by a WWF signpost. Follow the obvious tracks and paths through the forest and meadows. Be sure to bring plenty of insect repellent; during the summer months the onslaught of mosquitoes and other biting insects can be quite fierce.

One of the first things you will notice as you enter the woodland is the colony of tree-nesting white storks. Keep your eyes open for black storks and for birds of prey circling over clearings in the woodland. An impressive range of breeding birds can be found in the Marchauen including herons, warblers, woodpeckers and golden orioles.

### Wienerwald (Vienna Woods)

Lying west of Vienna, the Wienerwald is an extensive forested area comprising mainly oak, beech and hornbeam. The woods are rich

---

### Apollo Butterfly

The Apollo is one of the largest and most conspicuous butterflies found in the Alps. It is also commonly seen on Hohe Wand but lives only at the higher altitudes of the plateau summit.

Compared with many species of butterfly it is not a particularly active insect, and delights in basking in the sun. This characteristic behaviour is best observed in the evening as the butterflies catch the last of the sun's rays. They are often quite docile in the sunlight and make easy photographic subjects. The caterpillars feed on houseleeks, a group of plants that live in mountainous areas.

---

in wildlife, with red squirrels, woodpeckers, flycatchers and birds of prey among the attractions. Spring flowers can be excellent and several species of orchids can be found later in the year.

There are numerous parking areas with trails and paths through the forest. In particular, try visiting Sparbach which lies 15½ miles (25km) south of Vienna. A 2-mile (3-km) nature trail starts 6 miles (10km) west of Mödling at Schnepfenstein and finishes at Heuberg Gate. Also the Lainzer Tiergarten (Lainzer Zoo) is worth visiting for its collection of animals, including wild boar, red deer and fallow deer.

### Schönnbrunn Palace

Situated in the heart of Vienna, the palace gardens make a superb place for combining a peaceful stroll with wildlife observation. Park outside the palace entrance and wander through the formal gardens and areas of semi-natural woodland. As you walk along the avenue of trees from the entrance towards the palace, look for flycatchers, which nest both in holes in the trees and in nest boxes provided as man-made alternatives. Two species occur here – red-breasted and collared flycatchers – the latter easily recognised by its striking black-and-white plumage. Many of the woodland birds are tame and will come to visitors for food.

### Traunsee

This lake is a good place to look for waterbirds. Traunsee is best viewed at its southern end: take route 158 east from Salzburg to

## PEACE AND QUIET

Bad Ischl and take the 145 to Ebensee at the southern end of the lake. Scan the margins and open water for great crested grebes and ducks including pochards and tufted ducks.

### Grossglockner

Grossglockner is one of the most accessible areas of high Alps in Austria. The area is at the centre of the Hohe Tauern National Park and boasts the Grossglockner Mountain (at nearly 12,500 feet – 3,800m, the highest in Austria) and the Pasterze, one of the most impressive glaciers in Europe. To reach the Grossglockner, take route 107 which climbs southwards from Bruck an der Grossglocknerstrasse. Near the top of the pass, follow signs to Franz Josefs Höhe and park in the large car parking areas provided. You may wish to stop en route to and from the pass to allow your car's engine and brakes to cool down. This also allows you to admire some

of the Alpine scenery and flora at lower elevations than the car park.

If you do not wish to subject your car to the stress of the journey (which may take one and a half to two and a half hours in each direction to and from the toll gates and the top of the pass), regular bus and coach services operate from Bruck to the hotel at Franz Josefs Höhe at Grossglockner. Having parked your car, you will probably want to take a stroll down to look at the glacier. When you reach the foot of the glacier, look out for rock thrushes – colourful red and blue birds – and wallcreepers which, as their name implies, creep over the dripping rock faces in search of insects.

From the car park, a path leads up the side of the glaciated valley. If you follow this you will soon be aware of Alpine marmots near the path as well as the colourful Alpine flowers that grow here.

### Alpine Chough

Alpine choughs are perhaps the most familiar birds of the Alps, both to summer visitors and to winter sports enthusiasts. They are quick to take advantage of scraps of food left by visitors and will often fearlessly approach to within a few feet. The bird has all-black plumage and a long, curved yellow bill. In flight, it is nosy and aerobatic, often rolling over and tumbling in mid-air. Invariably, they are seen in flocks numbering several dozen birds.

### Rauristal Valley

For a pleasant drive through scenic terrain in the Austrian Alps, try the Rauristal valley. A single road runs south from near Taxenbach on the road between Bruck an der Grossglockenstrasse and Lend. It passes through the village of Rauris and on to Wörth and Kolm Saigurn. There are hay meadows full of colourful flowers in spring and summer, and griffon vultures and golden eagles are sometimes seen overhead. Look for black

*Hairpin bends on Grossglockner*

redstarts – small black birds with red tails – around farm buildings and gardens.

## Krimml Waterfalls

With a drop of 1,300 feet (400m) these are the largest waterfalls in Europe. They are situated near the village of Krimml, on route 165 west from Bruck an der Grossglocknerstrasse in the direction of Innsbruck. There are plenty of footpaths and skiing facilities in the area.

## Untersberg

Just outside Salzburg, this mountain rises to 6,560 feet (2,000m). It can be reached by cable-railway to Geiereck, at over 5,900 feet (1,800m), from here the area can be explored on foot. The mountain is mainly limestone, a rock that supports a diverse Alpine flora.

### Alpine Marmot

These large, shaggy-coated rodents are perhaps the most endearing creatures found in the Alps. They live in semi-communal burrow systems on the high slopes. During the winter months, when the mountain tops are covered with snow and ice, the marmots hibernate in underground chambers. In the spring, when the snow melts, they wake up and can be seen cleaning out their burrows and basking in the sunshine. In the Grossglockner area, their only real enemy is the golden eagle. Marmots keep a wary eye on the skies for these large and majestic birds of prey. If one is spotted, a shrill, far-carrying whistle is made by the alarmed animal to warn other marmots of the danger.

## PEACE AND QUIET

### Patscherkofel

This is one of the most accessible mountains in the Innsbruck area and has a cable-car service which facilitates exploration of the area. Away from the most disturbed areas, the Alpine flora is rich and includes colourful displays of alpenrose, which is actually a species of rhododendron. As is the case with most Alpine areas visited by tourists, Alpine choughs are much in evidence and will readily come for scraps of food. A high mountain path, called the Tiroler Zirbenweg, runs from the cable-car station on Patscherkofel to the foot of the Glungezer Peak. In the tree line, close by, birds such as citril finches can be seen.

*Argiope bruennichi is an orb-web spider. Look for the web and its maker in late summer and autumn. It is always the female which catches the eye, since the male is tiny and undistinguished. He is frequently eaten by the female after mating.*

### Alpine Flowers

Austria's Alpine flowers are one of the great delights of a visit during the spring and summer months.

The extensive network of cable cars and ski-lifts offers easy access to the high tops, and almost anywhere you choose to visit is likely to be good. Alpine flowers have to endure a harsh and prolonged winter, often under several feet of snow. Their growing and flowering period is often brief as the winter snows take a long time to melt and often return again in the autumn. Alpine meadows, grazed during the summer months by cattle brought up from the sheltered valleys, are particularly colourful and full of cranesbills, bedstraws, bellflowers, orchids and many others. More hardy species, such as saxifrages and houseleeks, prefer bare rock ledges or scree slopes.

### Hafelekar

A cable car from Innsbruck provides easy access to the top of this mountain from where extended walks can be made through the Karwendel region. Birds frequently seen at the summit include Alpine choughs, Alpine accentors and snow finches. A snow finch on the ground could be mistaken for a house sparrow, but in flight the white wings with black tips make it easy to identify. There are also good populations of red deer, chamois and ibex.

# *Practical*

*This section includes food, drink, shopping, nightlife, accommodation, tight budget, special events etc*

## **FOOD AND DRINK**

Austrian food is an eclectic mix of dishes, many of which originated in neighbouring lands, such as Bohemia, Hungary and northern Italy, which were once part of the diverse Habsburg Empire. There are still regional variations.

In general, the food is heavy and sustaining – essential for activities like skiing but not necessarily healthy if taken in large quantities. The two most wickedly fattening items, appearing all too frequently on menus, are *Obers* or *Schlagobers* (cream), secretly added to sauces, and *Knödel* (dumplings) made with flour, bread, semolina or potatoes. Visitors should try to forget about calorie counting while on holiday in Austria.

Throughout the country, meals are taken quite early – lunch from about noon, dinner from around 18.00 hrs. The Austrians love their food and may even squeeze in an extra snack (*Jause* or *Brettljause*) between meals, consisting of bacon, sausage, bread and cheese, all cold. Some people also

find space for a *Kaffeejause* (coffee and cake).

A traditional breakfast (*Frühstück*) is a comparatively light meal, with just rolls (*Semmeln*) or black bread (*Schwarzbrot*) and jam or honey, accompanied by coffee, thus leaving plenty of space for the rest of the day's food. However, boiled egg, ham, cheese and sliced sausage are frequently served.

Lunch (*Mittagessen*) is the Austrians' main meal of the day and can consist of three or more courses, but similar menus are usually available in the evening too. If you take soup as a starter (*Vorspeise*), you will often find it is almost a meal in itself. Clear soups may be made more filling by the addition of strips of pancake (*Frittatensuppe*) or liver dumplings (*Leberknödelsuppe*), while the thicker, peppery *Gulaschsuppe* comes with large lumps of meat.

The main course (*Hauptspeise*) usually consists of meat, such as beef or pork, made into stews or schnitzels. *Rostbraten* is braised steak in onion sauce, *Rindsbraten* is roast beef in cream sauce and *Tafelspitz* is

## FOOD AND DRINK

boiled fillet of beef served with a chive or horseradish and apple sauce and *Röstkartoffeln* (roast potatoes). Veal (*Kalb*) often turns up on menus in the form of *Gefüllte Kalbsbrust* (stuffed breast of veal) or *Kalbsvögerl* (paupiettes of veal). Veal is also the basis of the classic *Wienerschnitzel*, a thin slice of veal coated with breadcrumbs. Other types of schnitzel are the *Holstein* (with a fried egg and anchovies on top) and *Cordon Bleu* (cheese and ham are rolled up in the veal). These days, schnitzels are sometimes made with pork instead as it is cheaper. Other pork dishes include *Schweinsbraten* (roast pork) and *Schweinshaxn* (roast knuckle) and are likely to be accompanied by *Semmelknödel* (bread dumpling).

Stews are very popular too (often called *gulasch* when paprika is used), made with any of the above meats or with venison (*Hirsch*), which can also be served as *Wildragout* (made with red wine sauce). Other game (*Wild*), such as hare, is served with a cream sauce (*Hasenrücken*) and boar and pheasant are seasonal fare which appear on menus in some regions.

*Geflügel* (poultry) is served in many forms: chicken comes as *Brathuhn* (roast) or *Backhendl* (fried in breadcrumbs). Minced meat is often used to stuff green peppers (*Gefüllte Paprika*) or to make a meat loaf fried in breadcrumbs (*Faschierte Leiberln* or *Karbonadeln*).

A range of dishes known as *Hausmannskost* (home cooking) which used to be traditional peasant fare, appears in country inns, and usually consists of large helpings of cold meats, with sausage and bacon. *Bauernschmaus* is a large platter with *Geselchtes* (smoked meat), roast pork, fried sausages and boiled ham, together with *Sauerkraut* and dumplings.

Visitors should be aware that Austrians enjoy eating offal. If you don't, avoid *Beuschel* (lung stew) as well as dishes with *Leber* (liver), *Herz* (heart) and *Nieren* (kidneys), though these can be delicious. *Blutwurst* is black pudding and a wide range of sausages is available, including *Frankfurters* and *Krainers* (thick slices served with mustard), which are also sold on hot dog stalls (*Würstelstand*).

As Austria has no coast, fish is limited to the freshwater varieties, such as *Forellen* (trout), *Karpfen* (carp) and *Zander* (perch).

Vegetables (*Gemüse*) play second fiddle to meats and are not particularly exciting. The commonest is *Sauerkraut* (cabbage), usually pickled and chopped. *Gemischter Salat* contains a mix of cooked and raw vegetables, such as cooked beans, carrots, beetroot and lettuce. A fresh lettuce salad is *Grüner Salat*.

The puddings (*Süssspeisen* – *Mehlspeisen* are hot ones) are delicious and, unfortunately for the figure-conscious, hearty. Dumpling fans can succumb to temptation again – these dumplings are finally dipped into sugared breadcrumbs –

# FOOD AND DRINK

and try ones filled with apricots (*Marillenknödeln*), plums (*Zwetschken*) and *Topfen-knödeln* (white cheese). Fresh fruit – apricots, plums, cherries – may be stewed to make a compote and served with ice cream or in pancakes (*Palatschinken*). These, too, are served with a variety of fillings. *Kaiserschmarren* is a thick, puffy pancake made with raisins, then shredded and coated with icing sugar; it may be served with stewed fruit, often plums. *Salzburger Nockerl* is a large soufflé.

*Apfelstrudels* are flaky and light, and many volumes have been written on *Torten* (Austrian cakes). Most famous is the *Sachertorte*, a dark, rich, heavy chocolate cake with matching icing and a layer of apricot jam inside, best served with whipped cream (*Schlagobers*). It originated from the hotel of that name, but has since been much modified. Other well-known cakes are *Linzer* (made of nuts with jam under a

*Culinary delights of Austria: Apfelstrudel and Sachertorte*

trellis design) and *Topfentorte* (cheesecake).

As a reaction against the large portions of *Hausmannskost*, a lighter type of cuisine has been introduced in some restaurants, still based on local produce, but using less fat and giving smaller helpings: the Vorarlberg region is a trendsetter in this regard. Vegetarian food is easily found in most towns and in the ubiquitous restaurant chain Wienerwald. Pizzas, burgers and other take-away foods are also easy to come by.

## Where to Eat and Drink

A restaurant, *Gasthof* or *Gasthaus* serves meals, as does a *Beisl* (a Viennese tavern). Coffee and cakes are served in cafés, *Konditorei* (primarily a pastry shop) and in Viennese coffee houses, where there is a much wider choice of coffee. Some also serve meals; they all serve alcohol. Sausage stalls

## FOOD AND DRINK

proliferate in towns and resorts; an *Imbissstube* is a snackbar. Alcohol is on sale from whatever time the establishment opens. As well as the places mentioned above you can also drink in a *Bierstüberl* (for beer) or a *Weinstüberl* (for wine). At *Heurigen* (see **Wine** box, page 35) you mainly drink wine, but bottles of beer may be on sale too. Beer gardens are very popular and usually large and noisy, while in older parts of towns, cellars have been turned into drinking places, which are lit by candles.

### Drink

Alcoholic drinks are widely available at all hours and from many places. Beer is mainly of the lager type (*Gösser*, *Schwechater*, *Märzen*) and is sold in bottles (*Flaschen*) or from the barrel (*vom Fass*). You can ask for a *Krügel* (half-litre) or a *Seidel* (one-third of a litre). Wine is not sold only by the bottle or glass, but also in jugs. If you want to sample the local wine, order an *Achtel* (an eighth of a litre – a glassful) or a *Viertel* (a quarter). House wine is *Offener Wein*, but you might find a *Gespritzter* (wine with soda water), a refreshing alternative.

Austria produces more white wine than red (see **Wine** box, page 35), the most widely available being the dryish *Grüner Veltliner*. The best advice to visitors who do not already have a favourite wine, is to try the regional speciality, which is likely to be both cheaper and fresher than one which has travelled across the country.

Distilled drinks such as *Schnapps* (sometimes with a very high alcoholic content) are good value. So are fruit brandies, called *Obstbrand* or *Obstler*. They include *Zwetschken* (plums), *Kirsch* (cherries) and *Marillen* (apricots). The fruits are made into liqueurs and fruit juices (*Apfelsaft* is apple juice). In winter, rum served with tea (*Jägertee*) is particularly warming, and so is *Glühwein* (mulled wine).

**Vienna's Naschmarkt**

## SHOPPING

If you want to dress in traditional Austrian style you can buy a Loden coat or jacket, usually in green, made of a thick woollen cloth and steam pressed, available in shops in major towns. Other typical Austrian clothes include felt hats, decorated with feathers, *Lederhosen* (leather shorts) and *Dirndl* costumes (bodices and skirts which vary locally). Traditional glass, ceramic and pottery items are widely sold. Look particularly for Gmundner ceramics, brightly decorated, with great attention to detail, or the lovely hand-painted Augarten porcelain. Lace, embroidered table linen and bags made of embroidered cotton or petit point make attractive gifts. Jewellery is often good value, delicately wrought and made of semi-precious stones and silver. Enamelled jewellery is also pretty. Weekly open-air markets are held in country towns and in Vienna the Saturday *Naschmarkt* (flea market) draws huge crowds. Before Christmas, *Christkindlmärkte* (Advent markets) are held which sell lots of pretty decorations and dried flower and straw arrangements. Edible or drinkable reminders of your Austrian visit might include fruit brandies and liqueurs, some in unusual flavours – *Zirbengeist* (pine cone brandy) or *Enziangeist* (gentian brandy). *Nougat* is really a type of chocolate truffle and *Mozartkugeln* are chocolates filled with marzipan.

A good range of coffee is on sale (ground or beans) and if you drink weak tea and find teabags too strong, you can buy a tea filter. There are also gourmet variety mustards. In Styria the speciality is pumpkin seed oil (*Kürbiskernöl*), used for dressing salads. It is widely available throughout Austria. Many shops sell products from bees – wax candles, honey and furniture polish.

## ACCOMMODATION

Tourism is of great importance to the Austrian economy, so the quality and maintenance of hotels are taken very seriously. Hotels, guest houses etc. are inspected regularly and given star ratings ranging from one (simple, applicable to pensions and inns) to five (luxury hotels); the more stars, the more expensive the accommodation. The rooms and facilities are thoroughly examined, along with the standard of service and the way the establishment is run. The number of staff speaking foreign languages, the quality of bed linen, crockery and cutlery and the frequency of laundry change are also scrutinised.

It is always wise to book accommodation in advance. However, if you are travelling outside the main season (see **Tight Budget** on page 108) it should not be difficult to find a hotel or private room in the countryside. You may end up in a modern chalet-style building with a large garden. Accommodation at a reasonable price is always hard to find in Vienna and Salzburg;

## ACCOMMODATION

the more central, the more expensive. Many older buildings have been modernised, but do not always have a lift. Stairs can be steep and awkward, so keep your luggage down to a minimum. You might get better value by staying outside these towns and spend a little time travelling in each day by public transport. Rooms in Anif, for example, south of Salzburg cost considerably less than those in Salzburg, and if you are visiting Vienna, you might find it cheaper to stay in Klosterneuberg to the north or Mödling to the south. At most hotels, there are good sports facilities – perhaps a gym, sauna, swimming pool and tennis court.

### Hotels

There are a few hotel groups in Austria, mostly used by tour operators. Two outstanding and stylish groups to try, if you can afford it, are the Romantik Hotels and the Schlosshotels. Romantik Hotels are part of an international chain which prides itself on the high quality of its food, and mostly occupies older buildings. The Schlosshotels do not stick exclusively to castles – they also occupy former monasteries and palaces – but are usually furnished with antiques. Both groups also offer a range of sports facilities. Two relevant publications from ANTO are *Romantik Hotels* and *Restaurants and Gotha Schlosshotels*.

Another publication which lists all hotels awarded three stars or more is *Hotels in Österreich*

(Hotels in Austria), available from the ANTO. Each regional tourist board publishes an accommodation guide (see **Tourist Offices** in the **Directory** for addresses) which also includes self-catering (see page 101). These guides give dates and prices during high and low seasons (see **Tight Budget** on page 108) and cost of full- or half-board or just bed and breakfast.

Hotel bookings can be made in advance to over 400 hotels via Austria On-Line, a computer database (tel: 0345-581126). They also book tickets for events and charge agency commission and a booking fee.

### Other places to stay

Apart from hotels, which serve all meals, you can stay at a *Hotel Garni* or a *Pension*; both provide bed and breakfast only. A *Gasthof* is a hotel with a restaurant, usually in a small town, and a *Gasthaus* or *Gästehaus* is a country inn with a few rooms. Many of these establishments are family run and you would be expected to stay for at least a few days and preferably for a week. Sometimes the cost of the first night is more than that of subsequent nights as an inducement to stay longer. *Saisonhotels* are student hostels (in Vienna, for example) which are used as hotels for the summer months. Anyone can stay there.

A large number of *Privatzimmer* (private homes) offer bed and breakfast and make themselves known easily by displaying a '*Zimmer frei*' sign. They have a high standard of cleanliness and it is usually possible to find one either by driving round and looking for the sign, or asking at the local tourist office. Your bedroom may be equipped with only a washbasin and you may have to share a bathroom and toilet with other guests. Baths and showers sometimes cost extra.

Austrian farmhouses also offer hospitality – tell ANTO which region you want to visit and ask for a list.

### Alpine Huts

In the mountains, you can stay in hotels at lower levels but usually only in mountain huts higher up – prices rise with the altitude. The level of comfort in the huts, run by Alpine clubs and open only in high summer, can be described as adequate (often in dormitories) rather than comfortable. Meals and bedding are generally provided. Visitors are asked to obey house rules, such as helping dispose of rubbish.

### Youth Hostels

Youth hostels cater for the young and not-so-young and are considerably cheaper than hotels and slightly less than pensions. There are about 100 in Austria, and if you plan to spend your holiday staying in them it is worth joining the Youth Hostelling Association (YHA) in your own country and then buying a card to join the international set up. The Austrian youth hostel organisation is Österreichischer Jugendherbergsverband, A-1010 Vienna, Schottenring 28. (tel: 533-5353).

### Self-catering

For a self-catering family holiday in a chalet on a mountain or by a lake, obtain the brochure *Austria Chalets Apartments* which lists over 1,000, mostly with colour photos and very full details. Self-catering accommodation is listed in separate regional and town brochures – just tell ANTO where you want to go and they will provide you with a list.

## CULTURE, ENTERTAINMENT AND NIGHTLIFE

Austria's cultural heritage, especially music, is a magnet to thousands of visitors. They come not only to pay homage to the land where many of the world's greatest composers lived and wrote outstanding music (often due to the Habsburg patronage) and

*The bright lights of Vienna*

where many first performances took place, but also to hear how today's famous singers and players are interpreting this music (see **Special Events** page 109). Other visitors who come to Austria primarily to relax and admire the scenery, or to travel around or indulge in sport will also find plenty of culture on offer – museums, art galleries, cinemas and music in less serious forms.

For an up-to-date list of what's on, get a copy of the monthly list of events (*Programm*) published for Vienna and Salzburg.

*Mozart performed in costume at the Vienna Concert House*

### Opera and Theatre

The opera and theatre season in Austria lasts from September until June although some Viennese theatres stay open in July and August too. The two opera houses in Vienna are the *Staatsoper* (state opera house) where every seat has its own light for following the score, and the smaller *Volksoper* which performs light opera; both houses also put on ballets. You will find that most people dress formally when going to the opera. Operas are performed out of doors at Schönbrunn in July and August.

Over 40 theatres put on plays in Vienna, ranging from classical

to the avant-garde, usually performed in German except at Vienna's *English Theatre*. Some of the capital's most attractive theatres include the *Burgtheater* and the *Schönbrunner Schlosstheater*; the *Theater an der Wien* puts on musicals. In Salzburg, puppets sing operas at the *Marionetten Theatre*.

## Music Alone

The official concert season runs from October until June but many concerts are held during the summer months. Concerts of all types, from classical through to rock, are held in churches, palaces, concert and village halls as well as in the open air. In many parks, especially in spa towns, regular afternoon concerts are held, often free.

In Vienna you could attend concerts every night – at nearly 40 different venues. The main concert halls in the capital are the *Konzerthaus* and the *Musikverein*, home of the Vienna Philharmonic Orchestra, which also plays for the Vienna State Opera.

Concerts in Salzburg are performed in lovely surroundings where Mozart once appeared – in the Marble Hall of the *Mirabell Palace* or the *Residenz* of the Prince Archbishops. Other venues include the *Fortress*, two Festival Halls and the *Mozarteum*.

## Music and Drink

Visitors who want to follow lighter evening pursuits will have no problem finding somewhere to relax or to be entertained. Live jazz and folk music is performed at many bars and cafés throughout Austria – find out from the local tourist office or your hotel. Music on a more intimate scale is provided by pianists at Vienna's *Konzertcafés*, playing mainly waltzes during the afternoon or evening in hotels, cafés and on the Walzerschiff *'DDS' Johann Strauss* on the Danube Canal. *Schrammelmusik* is typically Austrian – the accordion played by someone in Tyrolean costume – and is frequently heard in *Heurigen* (see page 98).

## Dancing

Music and dancing go hand in hand (or foot in foot) and the two are merrily combined on summer evenings at village festivals where the local people proudly wear their traditional dress (*Trachten*), often accompanied by the local brass band. Thigh-slapping *Schuplatter* dances are also performed with gusto, often after a few drinks at a *Heuriger*. Visitors who think of Vienna as the home of the waltz can watch, or even participate in this dance each afternoon in its *Stadtpark*, while the capital's New Year's Eve balls and pre-Lenten dances are glittering occasions attended mostly by local residents. At Vienna's two Dance Festivals in February and July/August, the world's most famous dancers perform and offer instruction. More information from Internationale Tanzwochen Wien, A-1091 Vienna, Postfach 155 (tel: 935558).

## Gambling

For a glamorous evening out, you could consider visiting one of Austria's 11 casinos. They can be found at Baden, Badgastein, Bregenz, Graz, Kitzbühel, Kleinwalsertal, Linz, Salzburg, Seefeld, Velden and Vienna and usually open from late afternoon. You must be formally dressed.

## Tickets

### In Vienna

Some tour operators will buy your tickets for you, but will then take a hefty agency commission fee for themselves (50 per cent in the case of Austria on-Line for the Spanish Riding School and the Vienna Boys' Choir) as well as a large administration fee.

Information about international festivals is available from the ANTO, and smaller events from local tourist offices.
If you apply for tickets from your own country, do not send any money.

### Staatsoper, Volksoper (Opera Houses)

Tickets for both opera houses, the Burgtheater and Akademietheater are hard to come by. You can make postal bookings three weeks before you set off, by writing to Bundestheaterverband, Goethegasse 1, A-1010 Wien, or by visiting the box office no earlier than seven days before the performance. Telephone bookings are accepted from credit card holders living outside Austria six days before (tel: 513-1513).

### Spanische Reitschule (Spanish Riding School)

A-1010 Wien, Hofburg. Full performances take place on Sundays at 10.45hrs and sometimes on a Wednesday evening at 19.00hrs; there are shorter performances which held on Saturdays, starting at 09.00hrs.
The riders go abroad on tour for 2 months each year, so check that they will be there before you book.
Written applications should be sent to the Spanische Reitschule (address above). Rehearsals are held daily, between Tuesday and Saturday from 10.00 to 12.00hrs. No reservations are accepted – you must book a tour or queue at 1 Josefsplatz, Door 2.

### Wiener Sängerknaben (Vienna Boys' Choir)

Burgkapelle, A-1010 Wien, Hofburg, Schweizerhof. Mass with this world-famous choir and members of the Hofmusikkapelle of the Hofburg takes place at 09.15hrs on Sundays from mid-September until mid-June.
Write several months in advance if you want tickets; there may be returns or free standing room if you queue at the box office from 17.00hrs the previous Friday.

### Wiener Festwochen (Vienna Festival)

Held during May and June, this Festival is an amalgam of plays, operas, concerts and exhibitions. The programme is available in January from the Vienna Tourist Board, A-1025 Vienna (tel: 211-140);

*Dancing in Vienna's Volksgarten*

more details from Wiener
Festwochen, A-1060 Vienna,
Lehargasse 11 (tel: 586-1676).
**Wiener Musik-Sommer
(Vienna Summer Music Festival)**
Held in July and August the
programme is available from
Vienna Tourist Board (address
above) and you can reserve a
ticket by writing to Wiener
Musik-Sommer, A-1082, Vienna,
Friedrich-Schmidt-Platz 5 (tel:
4000-8400) before 30th April.

**In Salzburg**
For the annual **Salzburger
Festspiele** (Festival) in July and
August, you can apply for tickets
to the Festival Hall,
Hofstallgasse 1, Salzburg from
November to January. Even
better write to the Austrian
Tourist Office in your country.
For **Mozart week** in late January
write to the Mozarteum,
Schwartzstrasse 26, Salzburg.

## WEATHER AND WHEN TO GO

In a land where nearly 70 per
cent of the surface is mountains
or hills, Austria's physical
appearance changes
dramatically from white to

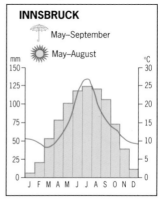

**INNSBRUCK**

May–September

May–August

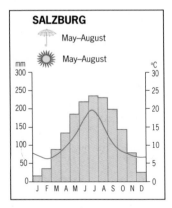

**SALZBURG**

May–August

May–August

green as the winter snow disappears. Visitors should be aware that many tourist attractions, gardens and buildings are closed during the winter.

Austria's climate is determined not only by its location in central Europe, but also by its mountains, which cool the atmosphere, bringing rain and snow. The flatter eastern part of the country has a more extreme climate. Snow can arrive in November and stay until April

but at higher altitudes lies for longer.

The busiest holiday period in the summer is mid-July to mid-August; it is also the most expensive. (See **Tight Budget** on page 108) The most pleasant months for most of the country are May (when the mountains burst forth with spring flowers), June and September, the driest month. Salzburg is notorious for rain and although the city can look lovely under snow, many mountains are covered up and buildings closed. Vienna can be even colder than Salzburg in winter.

## HOW TO BE A LOCAL

Wherever you go, you will receive a warm welcome (*Grüss Gott!*), for hospitality is an important national characteristic. This welcome owes much to the famous Austrian *Gemütlichkeit* (cosiness), and is prevalent not only in homes, but also in drinking places such as *Stuben* and *Heurigen*, where jollity often begins early in the evening. You may find that you are so comfortably looked after that your travel plans fade away and you decide to stay put, for accommodation standards are high, both in cleanliness and service. These two traits percolate through to the towns – well-swept streets and newly painted buildings, and plenty of flower displays to add yet more colour. Public transport is astonishingly efficient and punctual, even in the bad weather, and the scenery is often better than the picture books portray.

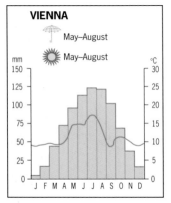

**VIENNA**

May–August

May–August

The Austrians' reputation of being fond of food and drink is true. Health is always an important conversation topic and the country's numerous spas continue to flourish as Austrians swarm there to be cured.

Young people are as lively and frivolous as elsewhere in Western Europe, and dress informally, but the older generation tend to be much more formal. In Vienna, many an elderly lady sets out wearing a hat and gloves to meet her friends for afternoon coffee and cake. Formal dress is definitely the order of the evening at the opera and at the first night at music festivals. In the countryside you will notice that families dress up on Sundays, and people walking on the mountains are always correctly kitted out.

Austria is now facing problems with the influx of refugees from Eastern Europe and the former Soviet Union. But with a strong sense of hospitality and earlier experience of hosting the homeless there is no doubt that they will cope admirably.

## CHILDREN

If the weather is warm, children will be very happy spending their holidays in Austria. Although there is no sea, the lakes and beaches provide a huge play area if they enjoy water sports and are well supervised, but the water can be cold (see **Sport** page 110). Large, stuffy museums, worthy but not child-friendly, should be avoided. Open-air museums however, and houses where famous composers lived are

*Water-play is serious business*

## CHILDREN/TIGHT BUDGET

likely to appeal, as will the Marionette Theatre in Salzburg. Children will enjoy gameparks and zoos and exploring natural features such as mountains, by cog-railway, cable car or on foot, lakes on boats, or visits down caves and salt mines. Trips on steam railways are always popular. A useful list appears in the brochure *Facts and Sights* published by ANTO. Many hotels and pensions give reductions to children sharing their parents' room and provide special facilities for them such as a playground or games room. Restaurants often provide special children's menus and there is no restriction on taking children into licensed cafés, *Heurigen* or restaurants. *Vorarlberg* does a lot for children: it puts on a special programme *Vorarlberg Children's Wonderland* in July and August in every resort, with over 200 events including

*Corpus Christi is celebrated in colourful local costumes*

sports, hobby afternoons and adventure hikes; highlights include the Giant Chocolate Festival in *Bludenz*. *Vorarlberg* also has a 'Family Club', scheme in which nearly 40 hotels and restaurants participate. Apart from games and a swimming pool, the hotels provide babysitting services, children's meals and discounts, and a family activity programme. Further information in the *Family Club* brochure available from Vorarlberg Tourismus, PO Box 302, Römerstrasse 7, A-6901 Bregenz. Mayrhofen and Söll also run children's programmes – ask for the ANTO brochure *Activity Holidays in Austria*.

### TIGHT BUDGET

● The cost of accommodation varies according to the

weather, and many Austrian resorts have two high holiday seasons, (*Hauptsaison*), one in summer and one in winter. If you do not want to pay the maximum, you should go either before the main season (*Vorsaison*), or after it (*Nachsaison*), which, confusingly, vary from region to region. In some regions, Carinthia for example, there is also an 'in between season' (*Zwischensaison*) price. Generally, July and August are the most expensive months.

● The price of accommodation also varies according to location, and it is usually cheaper to stay in the countryside than in towns where room prices are the same all year. Rooms cost less without a bath or shower. Some university accommodation is made available for summer tourists, but it may be dormitory-type.

● Travel is cheaper if you buy a special ticket (see **Directory**).

● For culture, you may get into museums free and can hear free concerts in public parks and frequently be entertained by street musicians.

● In warm weather make up picnic meals. Entry to the EU has brought down food prices, but not in restaurants.

● If the weather is cold, you can easily buy a sustaining *Gulaschsuppe* and roll.

● *Table d'hôte* (set priced) meals are cheaper than those *à la carte*, but pizzas, take-aways and sausages are cheaper still.

● If you are *really* hard pressed then avoid coffee and cakes which are expensive.

## SPECIAL EVENTS

International music festivals, many on a grand scale, take pride of place among Austria's special events, but concerts and operas are performed in many small towns and villages, often devoted to one composer. The larger the festival, the earlier you need to book tickets – up to a year in advance. The ANTO has lots of information. Below is a selection, but more will be found in the ANTO brochure *A Country Made for Holidays*.

**February**: Fasching (Carnival)
**March**: Vienna Viennale (Film Festival)
**Easter**: Salzburg Easter Festival
**Late April to mid-May**: Bregenz Spring Festival
**Early May to mid-June**: Wiener Festwochen (Vienna Festival)
**Mid-May to late October**: Eisenstadt Haydn Concerts
**Late May to mid-June**: St Pölten Festival
**Mid-June to late September**: Viennaklangbogen (Summer Music Festival)
**June**: Baden Rose Days. Ebensee, Traunsee, Hallstatt – Corpus Christi processions
**Mid to late June**: Feldkirch – Schubertiade Hohenems (Schubert Festival)
**Late June**: Salzburg area (Zederhaus, Muhr) – Prangstangen processions
**Late June to early August**: Innsbruck Ambras Palace concerts
**End-June to end-July**: Zwettl Abbey International Organ Festival
**End-June to early September**: Baden Operetta Summer

## SPECIAL EVENTS/SPORT

**Early July to early August**:
Melk Summer Festival
**July to August**: Millstatt
International Music Festival
**Last week July**: Villach Folklore
Week
**Late July to late August**:
Bregenz Festival
**Late July to late August**:
Salzburg International Festival
**August (first 2 weeks)**:
Hellbrunn Festival
**Beginning August to beginning
September**: Gmunden Festival
**September**: Linz International
Bruckner Festival
**Early September**: Eisenstadt
Haydn Festival
**September, October**: Baden
Beethoven Festival
**Mid- to end-September**:
St Johann Alpine Pasture Festival
**End-September to
end-October**: Graz Styrian
Autumn Festival

## SPORT

Austria is not only ideal for a
winter sports holiday, but for a
summer one too. Many resorts
and individual hotels offer a
range of sports facilities –
tennis, table tennis, golf, riding,
swimming pool, fitness centre
(a gym) and cycle hire –
sometimes included in the hotel
price, sometimes extra.
At lakeside resorts, a range of
water sports – sailing,
windsurfing, fishing – is
available, as well as games like
tennis and golf. If you are keen
to do a particular sport, ask the
local tourist office.
If you would like to have a go at
something new, try the 'Europe
Sport Region', based at the
lakeside resort of Zell am See

(for watersports) and the village
of Kaprun (for mountain
pursuits). The Mount Alpine
adventure programme offers a
combination of over 30
activities. (Information from
local tourist offices – A-5700
Zell am See or A-5710 Kaprun.)
The useful ANTO publication
*Activity Holidays in Austria* is full
of ideas.
Older visitors preferring less
active sports might consider
staying at a spa, where many
pursuits, apart from the curative
water treatments, are available.
The brochure *Nature the Healer*
lists spas, sports and the most
beneficial type of water for
each ailment.

### Cycling

The ANTO publishes a leaflet
*Cycling in Austria* which lists
several routes and tour
operators who offer cycling
holidays. Organised tours (you
travel with your friends, not in a
group) include hire of bike, a
route map, transfer of luggage
and accommodation and meals
booked in advance. A discount
is often given for children.
There are about 5,000 miles
(8,000km) of tracks along easy
lowlands to more difficult routes
in the Alps. One fairly level
route, suitable for beginners, is
along the Danube from Passau
to Hainburg (217 miles/350km).
A harder route is in the
Mühlviertel area, along the
Czech and Bavarian borders.
The intrepid can hire mountain
bikes or bring their own; riders
should also bring their own
helmets. Guided tours are
available in most areas.
Bicycles can be hired from

railway stations and you can get a 50 per cent reduction if you hire a bike the same day you arrive (see also page 121).

### Fishing

The comprehensive booklet *Austria's Fishing Waters* lists lakes and streams, the fish you can catch, the name of local fishing experts and the cost of permits (daily or weekly). It also gives prices of fishing holidays (permit cost included).

### Golf

Over 60 golf courses and hotels are listed in the booklet *Courses and Hotels in Austria*. The golf hotels are usually situated close to several courses and the package holidays they offer include green fees on different courses and lessons for beginners and experts; the cost of balls is often excluded. Players wanting an occasional

*Golf is becoming increasingly popular in Austria*

game can easily get information from the local tourist office.

### Mountains

One of Austria's main attractions offers great challenges in a variety of sporting activities. If you are inexperienced, get advice or a guide before setting off and ensure your equipment is in good order. Always tell someone where you are going. Rock and ice climbing, abseiling and summer skiing on glaciers should only be carried out under instruction. The Alpine School at **Lech** or the mountaineering schools in the **Ötztal valley** are good places to start learning. (Information from tourist offices at A-6764 Lech am Arlberg or Ötztal Arena, A-6450 Sölden).

## SPORT

### Riding
*Reiten in Österreich* (Riding in Austria), written in German and well illustrated, lists establishments offering riding holidays, the number of horses and the type of riding – jumping, trekking etc.
Riding for a day or half day is possible at many resorts and usually indicated in hotel listings.

### Rock climbing
See **Mountains**, page 111.

### Tennis
Keen tennis players can stay at special Tennishotels or Tenniscamps, generally set amid lovely mountain scenery, where you can take lessons and play games. Most places offer other sports too. Ask for the comprehensive brochure

*Spectacular skiing at Zell am See*

*Tennis in Österreich* (Tennis in Austria).

### Walking
Most hilly and mountain areas have well-marked paths, with signposts telling you the distance and time to reach your destination. Proper clothing and footwear are advisable; tell someone where you are heading for.
If you are going on a mountain walking holiday, it might be worth joining the ÖAV, *Österreichischer Alpenverein* (Austrian Alpine Club – branches in most countries or enquire at the ANTO). A comprehensive list of addresses and hiking routes is given in the free Tirol brochure (see **Tourist Offices** in Directory).

### Watersports
With over 2,000 lakes of varying sizes, it is difficult to decide where to go. On many lakes – **Achensee, Attersee, Bodensee, Mondsee, Weissensee, Wörthersee, Neusiedlersee, Traunsee,** and **Wolfgangsee** – a range of watersports such as sailing, surfing and water-skiing take place and lessons are available. The publication *Wassererlebnis Österreich* (Austrian Water Experience) in German provides lots of information including the addresses of the schools.
River rafting is popular at St Johann in Tirol and canoeing in the Ziller river and on the Hallstätter See.
Tamer pursuits, like swimming, diving, hiring a rowing boat, or sun-bathing on the *Strandbad* (beach) can also be enjoyed.

# *Directory*

*This section contains day-to-day information, including travel, health and documentation.*

## Contents

## Arriving

### By Air
International airlines fly into Graz, Innsbruck, Linz, Klagenfurt, Salzburg, and Vienna. The Austrian air companies are Austrian Airlines, Lauda Air and Tyrolean Airways. Airbuses connect the airports with the railways stations and town centres. Travelling to Western Austria, you can use Munich or Zurich airports too. If you plan to fly to Austria and hire a car, it is likely to be cheaper to book this type of holiday through a travel agent in your own country.

### By Rail
Österreichische Bundesbahnen (ÖBB) (Austrian Federal Railways) run a reliable and frequent service which has a network across the whole country and links internationally with all European countries (see **Public Transport**).

### By Road
Drivers entering Austria need no customs documents for their cars. A national driving licence and registration documents will be enough. Vehicles must have third party insurance cover.

### By Boat
From April to October it is possible to arrive in Vienna by

## DIRECTORY

boat along the Danube from
Bratislava and Budapest.
Services operated by DDSG
(tel: 222-727100)

### Entry Formalities
No visa is necessary to enter
Austria, only a valid passport.
There are now lengthy border
checks on Eastern frontiers.

### Camping and Caravanning
The Austrian Tourist Board
publishes a large map showing
the country's 500 campsites. It
also provides much detailed
information, including dates of
opening, phone numbers and
facilities, such as size of plot,
amount of shade from trees and
provision of laundry,
restaurants and showers.
If you plan to go somewhere
high, you should check routes
with a motoring organisation as
many passes and mountain
roads are rather precipitous or
narrow for a trailer and some
are actually closed to them.
You can camp outside official
sites if you obtain permission
from the landowner. You may
also sleep in a caravan, except
in Vienna and in protected rural
areas, but you are not allowed
to set up a tent by your car
wherever you choose.

### Crime
Austria is less crime-ridden
than many European countries.
In rural areas people often do
not lock their homes. However,
visitors to towns should still take
care of their valuables – keep
money and documents close to
you in a purse or money belt.
Never leave luggage
unattended or visible in a car.

### Customs Regulations
Visitors can bring in cameras,
video recorders, tennis rackets
and other items for their own
use. Each visitor over 17 years
of age can also bring in duty
free 200 cigarettes (or 50 cigars
or 250g tobacco), 2.25 litres of
wine and 1 litre of spirits. Items
for *personal use* can be
imported from one EU country
to another without payment of
duty, although maximum limits
have been established for
cigarettes, cigars, wines, spirits
and perfumes.

### Travellers with Disabilities
Each province in Austria
publishes a list of hotels suitable
for people with disabilities; ask
the ANTO (Austrian National
Tourist Office) for a copy. Many
hotels adapted for those with
disabilities have a special
symbol.
The Vienna Tourist Board
publishes a guide to hotels
adapted for people with
disabilities, and a city map
showing which sights are
accessible to wheelchair users.
The Organisation for the
Disabled in Austria is *Verband
aller Körperbehinderten
Österreichs*, Lützowgasse 24–8,
Stiege 3, A-1140, Vienna. The
association of wheelchair users
is *Verband der Querschnitts-
gelähmten Österreichs*,
Liechtenstein-strasse 57, A1090
Vienna.

### Driving
Drive on the right. All cars must
carry a first aid kit and warning
triangle. Maximum speed limits
are 81mph (130km) on
motorways, 62mph (100km) on
trunk roads and 30mph (50km)

*Indulge yourself – try chocolate shopping in Karntnerstrasse, Vienna*

in towns. If towing a trailer heavier than ¾ of a ton, the limit is 50mph (80km) on main roads and 62mph (100km) on motorways.

Seatbelts are compulsory and children under 12 may not sit in the front seat.

An excellent map of Austria (*Facts and Sights*), free from the ANTO, lists all the Alpine passes, their altitudes and gradients and also toll roads and the cost of using them. See **Media** for traffic news.

### Accidents and breakdowns

If you have an accident, you must report it at once to the police (tel: 133) if someone is injured. The 24-hour emergency breakdown services can be used by anyone: ÖAMTC (tel: 120) or ARBÖ (tel: 123).

### Alcohol

If you are found to be over the limit of 80mg alcohol per 100ml blood, you can be fined up to AS 8000 and have your licence confiscated.

### Car Rental

It is easy to hire a car in Austria from an independent company or from a large international one. You have to have held a licence for at least a year and be 18 years old to hire a small car, 21 to hire a larger one. You can pay with a credit card.

### Fuel

Unleaded petrol (*Bleifrei*) with 91 octanes is the regular grade, while the 95-octane grade is called Eurosuper or Euro-95. Petrol with a lead substitute is also available.

### Lights

Drivers from the UK must adjust their headlamp beams. All drivers must have lights on in tunnels.

### Motoring Organisations

OAMTC (Österreichischer Automobil, Motorrad- & Touring Club), Schubertring 1–3, A1010 Wien (tel: 1-711

## DIRECTORY

*Keeping up with the news*

990) and ARBO (Auto, Motor & Radfahrerbund Österreichs), Mariahilfer-strasse 80, A 1150 Wien (tel: 853535).

### Mountain Driving
When descending a road with a very steep gradient, make sure you engage in a low gear early. The edges of most mountain roads are fitted with guard rails (see **Snowy conditions** below).

### Parking
Some towns have blue zones where you can park for up to three hours. You must display a disc, resembling a clock, in your windscreen. These are obtainable, free, from tobacconists' shops (*Tabak-Trafik*). In a few towns you have to buy parking vouchers (*Park Scheine*) from banks, petrol stations and tobacconists. It is particularly difficult to park in Salzburg.

### Snowy Conditions
You must use winter tyres on snowy surfaces; studded tyres can be used from 15th November to the first Sunday after Easter. Both types can be hired from the motoring organisations (see page 115). In extreme conditions, snow chains must be used.

### Electricity
Electric current is 220 volts AC and appliances need two-pin, continental plugs.

### Embassies and Consulates
**American Embassy,**
Boltzmanngasse 16,
A-1090 Vienna.
Tel: (222) 31339

**Australian Consulate,**
Mattiellistrasse 2–4,
A-1040 Vienna.
Tel: (222) 512 8580/512 9710

**British Embassy,**
Jauregasse 12,
A-1030 Vienna.
Tel: (222) 75 61 17 or 18
Outside office hours: 713 15 75

**Canadian Embassy,**
Lourenzerburg 2,
A-1010 Vienna.
Tel: (222) 531 380

**Irish Embassy,**
Landstrasser Haupstr.2,
Hilton Center, Postfach 139,
16 Stock, A-1030 Vienna.
Tel: (222) 75 42 46

### Emergency Telephone Numbers
Ambulance 144
Fire 122
Police 133
Driving breakdown 120 or 123

## Health

No inoculation is needed to enter Austria. It is advisable to take out travel insurance. British visitors should obtain form E111 from a post office to benefit from reciprical health facilities in Austria. Although any stay in hospital is free, you will have to pay for treatment and medication, as well as any doctor's fees if you are ill. In most towns, a medical emergency service (*Ärztenotdienst*) is available – ask at the police station or local chemist. Mountain resorts have their own rescue teams (*Bergrettungdienst*).

The water is drinkable everywhere. See also **Pharmacies**.

## Holidays

On the days listed below, banks and public buildings are closed as well some museums; others may open for restricted hours.
New Year's Day – 1 January
Epiphany – 6 January
Easter Monday
Labour Day – 1 May
Ascension Day
Whit Monday
Corpus Christi
Assumption – 15 August
National Holiday – 26 October
All Saints' Day – 1 November
Immaculate Conception – 8 December
Christmas Day – 25 December
St Stephen's Day – 26 December
Schools' half-term holidays are taken in the first three weeks in February and the summer holidays from early July to mid-September. One week's holiday is also taken at Easter.

## Lost Property

Report any loss to the police station, where you will be asked to fill in a form. If there is a local lost property office, they will tell you. There is a good chance that you will retrieve anything which you have lost.

## Media

Austrian Radio broadcasts news bulletins in English and French on the first programme (Ö1) every day from 08.05 to 08.15hrs. The BBC World Service broadcasts in English very early (06.00 to 07.30hrs) on 15.575MHz.

The Austrian radio station Ö3 broadcasts traffic news after each hourly news bulletin – in German – about weather, accidents and traffic jams. Blue Danube Radio broadcasts in English, French and Spanish. It transmits traffic news in English between 07.00 and 09.00hrs, noon and 14.00hrs, and if there are serious delays, also between 18.00 and 19.30hrs (103.8 MHz in Vienna area, 101.4 MHz in Innsbruck).

English newspapers are widely available at railway stations and news stands in large towns and resorts.

## Money Matters

The unit of currency is the Austrian *Schilling* (AS) denominated in notes of 20, 50, 100, 500 1000 and 5000 and in coins of 1, 5, 10 and 20. The *Schilling* is divided into 100 *Groschen* issued in coins of 2, 5, 10 and 50, which these days are worth very little. You can bring as much currency into and out of Austria as you wish.

## DIRECTORY

Travellers' cheques can be exchanged at banks, hotels and bureaux de change, but you need to watch the commission charged. Credit cards (Visa and Mastercard) and charge cards (Diners and Amex) are accepted by hotels, restaurants and some garages.

### Taxes
Austria seems to impose a lot of small taxes, some of which you will pay without knowing, and others which you should be aware of. A local and regional tax, varying from area to area, is added on to the accommodation bill. This tax often entitles you to a visitors' card (*Gästekarte*) with which you get a discount on local entertainment and sporting activities. In spa towns, too, a tax may be incurred and visitors receive a similar ticket (*Kurkarte*) for local discounts.

### VAT refunds
Since Austria joined the European Union, VAT refunds are available only to non-EU citizens. Non-EU members can obtain refunds on single purchases worth more than AS 1,000.

### Mountains
For fine views and excellent walking, remember that Austria has several means of transport up mountains – chair lifts, cog railways and cable cars. Most operate in summer as well as for skiing.

### Opening Times
Most shops open Monday to Friday from 08.00hrs to 18.30hrs with a one- or two-hour lunch break. On Saturdays they stay open to 13.00hrs. These hours are flexible throughout the country, and in summer, many shops stay open later.

Banks open Monday to Friday 08.00 to 12.30hrs and 13.30 to 15.00hrs. In Vienna, banks open late on Thursdays (to 17.30hrs). Banks do not open on Saturdays. You can exchange money outside these hours at Vienna's two main railway stations – from 06.30 to 22.00hrs at Südbahnhof and from 07.00 to 22.00hrs at Westbahnhof – and at the City Air Terminal (08.00 to 12.30hrs and 14.00 to 18.00hrs). Schwechat airport has exchange facilities open from 06.30 to 23.00hrs.

Museums are usually open Monday to Friday from 10.00 to 18.00hrs in the summer and 09.00 to 16.00hrs in the winter. Weekends and public holidays: 09.00 to 18.00hrs. However, you should check in advance. In Salzburg and Vienna, many museums close on Mondays.

Post offices are generally open Monday to Friday, 08.00hrs to noon and 14.00 to 18.00hrs; on Saturdays, many are open from 08.00 to 10.00hrs. In larger cities, the main post office is open 24 hours a day, including weekends and public holidays.

### Pharmacies
Chemists' (*Apotheken*) operate a rota system and one is always open at nights and on Sundays.

### Places of Worship
About four-fifths of the Austrian population is Catholic, and every small village has a Catholic church, chapel or shrine for worship. In Carinthia

and Styria there is a concentration of Protestant churches. The country's only Muslim mosque is in Vienna, where there is also a synagogue.

### Police

Austrian police are polite and helpful. The traffic police are separate from the criminal police. Dial 133 for assistance.

### Post Office

See **Opening Times** opposite. Postage stamps are sold at post offices and at tobacco kiosks. Some letter boxes are yellow, some orange.

### Public Transport

Austria runs an efficient public transport system with well-coordinated timetables of buses and trains.

### Air

Internal flights are operated by Austrian Air Services between Graz, Innsbruck, Klagenfurt, Linz, Salzburg and Vienna and by Tyrolean Airways from Innsbruck. Further information from Austrian Airlines in your own country.

### Rail

Trains run by Österreichische Bundesbahnen (ÖBB – Austrian Federal Railways) travel the length and breadth of the country, offering speed, comfort and wonderful scenery. Some lines, however, mainly with a stock of steam trains, are still privately owned, and chug around lakes and along valleys.

*There are many wayside shrines to be seen in Austria, such as this at Faaker See*

# DIRECTORY

*View Vienna by tram. If you use the Vienna Card, you travel free*

The ÖBB also operates two cog railways and boats on the Wolfgangsee and on the River Danube. More information from the useful booklet *Servus in Austria with the Railways* from the Tourist Office.

In Vienna, the Vienna Card provides free travel on the public transport network for 3 days and discounts for 4 days on concerts, museums, restaurants and shops. Obtainable from hotels and tourist offices.

## Trains

EuroCity trains (which also serve European cities outside Austria) travel at speeds up to 160km per hour and stop only at major cities; others which stop less frequently are called SuperCity trains. You have to pay a special supplement to travel on these trains. InterCity trains operate at hourly or two-hourly intervals. Slower, local trains also run.

Steam train addicts will enjoy riding on some of the private railways on the Achensee, Zillertal or Montafon lines. The brochure *Nostalgie-Sonderfahrten* details these and other 'romantic' railways.

## Tickets

Ordinary tickets are valid for one day if the journey is less than 70km, up to 4 days if it is more, but a wide variety of discounted tickets is available. A *Nahverkehrs-Rückfahrtkarte* (short-trip return ticket) is valid for four days for an unlimited number of journeys up to 70km. A Puzzle ticket, first or second class, entitles you to 4 days travel throughout Austria within a 10-day period, while a *Bundes-Netzkarte* (National Rail Pass) offers the same benefits on all of Austria's 18 different rail regions.

Two tickets which visitors must buy in their home country allow unlimited travel around Austria. One is **Inter Rail** (which also lets you ride on the Schneeberg and Schafberg cog railways at half-price) and the other is the **Euro-Domino** ticket, enabling the holder to travel anywhere in Austria for 3, 5 or 10 days within one month.

Non-European visitor's can buy a **Eurail Pass**, giving first-class unlimited travel in Europe, and a **European East Pass** for travel within the Czech Republic, Slovakia, Poland and Hungary, as well as Austria.

Children under six not occupying a seat travel free; six to 15 year-olds pay half fare.

### Bicycles

Bicycles can be hired at over 140 railway stations in Austria – you can return the bike to another station – and take them on certain trains. Ask the Tourist Office for the brochure *Fahrradprospekt* and see cycling in the **Sports** section (page 110).

### Cars

Cars can be hired at some stations and can be taken on the motorail – ask for the leaflet *Autoreisezüge*.

If you do not fancy driving over the Alps, you can use the shuttle service (*Autoschleuse Tauernbahn*) through the tunnel between Böckstein station (tel: 6434-266 339) and Mallnitz-Obervellach (tel: 4784-23033).

(See also **Senior Citizens** and **Student and Youth Travel**, page 122).

### Buses

Bus and coach services also have a good network throughout the country, operated by local and federal authorities as well as by private companies.

All services are efficient and clean. Buses are cheaper than trains and tend to take a bit longer, but they go to more outlying areas which trains cannot reach, as do the delightful local post buses.

### Boats

The Danube is used for passenger travel from April to October between Passau, Vienna and Budapest. More information is in the brochure *Bahn, Bus, Schiff* from a tourist office or railway station.

Between May and September, boats operated by ÖBB ply Lake Constance (Bodensee) and the Wolfgangsee.

A pass for Lake Constance gives unlimited boat travel for seven days during a 15-day period. The Euro-Domino and Eurail passes include reductions for boat trips on these lakes. (See also **Mountains**, page 118).

### Taxis

Fares are metered, but you should also offer a tip of 10 per cent of the cost. In Vienna, where taxis are hard to find, as well as the kilometre (metered) charge, you pay a basic charge, and a surcharge for luggage over 20kg, for travelling on Sundays, bank holidays or after 23.00hrs and for going to the airport. They are not metered for trips outside Vienna.

# DIRECTORY

## Senior Citizens

A Rail Europe Senior card entitles European residents over 60 to a 30 per cent discount on Austrian trains. To obtain this, you must first buy a Senior railcard in your own country and then pay a little extra for the European one. Information can be obtained from your nearest mainline station. The age limit may vary from country to country. Some museums may offer concessions to the over-60s.

## Student and Youth Travel

Some good travel discounts are available to young people under 26. The Eurail Youth Pass can be bought by young people living outside Europe (they must buy the pass in their home country) and gives them second-class rail travel in Europe for one or two months. Two tickets on sale to young people who live in Europe and want to see their own continent from a train are the Inter Rail Junior ticket, valid for a month, and the Euro-Domino Junior ticket valid for five days within any month. More information can be obtained from main stations in your own country. Museums give discounts to students on presentation of a student card, and so do some theatres and concerts. Cheap accommodation is available in Youth Hostels (write to the head office in your own country to get an international card). The head office in Austria is Österreichischer Jugendherbergsverband, Schottenring 28, A-1010 Vienna (tel: 1-533 5353).

Ask for the useful publication *Youth Scene – Szene* which provides lots of information about Vienna – where to stay, what to see, and where to eat, drink and dance.

## Telephones

Phone booths abound and accept coins or a phone card (*Wertkarte*) which you can buy from a post office or tobacco kiosk.

Public phones begin charging as soon as you start to dial and you should be able to get your money back if no-one answers, as long as there is change in the machine. It is best to put small denomination coins in at first. Making phone calls from a hotel can be very expensive – go to a main post office if you want to make a long-distance call. Calls are 35 per cent cheaper between 18.00 and 08.00hrs and at weekends from Friday at 18.00 until Monday at 08.00hrs. Telephone numbers in Austria are constantly changing due to modernisation, so try to check the number before dialling. When making an internal phone call within Austria, you must dial 0 first. For directory enquiries (within Austria) dial 1611 and for queries about numbers abroad, dial 1614.

Codes for dialling out of Austria are:

to Australia – 0061
to Canada and USA – 001
to UK – 0044
to Ireland – 00353

To phone Austria from the UK, dial 0043 followed by the town code and number. The town code for Vienna is 1 from abroad, 222 when in Austria.

## Time

Austria is on Central European Time, one hour ahead of GMT, 6 hours ahead of New York and 9 hours behind Sydney.

## Tipping

Service in restaurants is usually included, but it is usual to give a small tip. You should give about 10 per cent to taxi drivers and 5 per cent to hairdressers, but you should also give something to the person who washes your hair. Cloakroom (coats) and lavatory attendants should also be given a small tip.

## Toilets

Austrian toilets are generally immaculately cleaned and properly maintained and well worth the few *Schillings* you may be asked to pay. The sexes are indicated by *Herren* and *Damen* or by pictograms.

## Tourist Offices

Every town and village has its tourist office, which go under a variety of long names – *Verkehrsvereine*, *Fremdenverkehrsamt*, *Fremdenverkehrsverband* or *Turismusverband*. In spa towns you may come across *Kurkommissionen* (spa offices). Opening hours are quite long in summer and the offices provide plenty of free brochures and maps (*Stadtplan* is a town map). Tourist offices, will not book accommodation for you although they may direct you to a hotel booking agent who will – for a small fee (see also page 99).

*Dining out in Kärntnerstrasse*

## Accommodation

The brochure *A Country Made for Holidays* has the addresses of the tourist offices in the nine federal republics in Austria.

## Burgenland

Landfremdenverkehrsverband für das Burgenland, A-7000 Eisenstadt, Schloss Esterhozy. Tel: (2682) 63384

## Kärnten (Carinthia)

Kärntner Tourismusgesellschaft m.b.H., Casinoplatz 1, A-9220 Velden. Tel: (4274) 52100

## Niederösterreich (Lower Austria)

Niederösterreich Tourismus Werbung, Hoher Harht, A-1014 Wien. Tel: (1) 533 3114

## DIRECTORY

**Oberösterreich
(Upper Austria)**
Landesverband für Tourismus
in Oberösterreich,
Schillerstrasse 50,
A-4010 Linz.
Tel: (732) 6002210

**Salzburger Land**
Salzburger Land-Tourismus
Ges. m. b. H.,
Postfach 1,
Hallwang bei Salzburg
A-5033 Salzburg,
Tel: (662) 66880

**Steiermark (Styria)**
Steiermark Werbung,
St Peter Hauptstrasse 293,
A-8042 Graz.
Tel: (316) 40 30 330.

**Tirol (Tyrol)**
Tirol Werbung,
Bozner Platz 6,
A-6010 Innsbruck.
Tel: (512) 5320 59.

**Vorarlberg**
Vorarlberg-Tourismus,
Römerstrasse 7/1,
A-6901 Bregenz.
Tel: (5574) 42525-0.

**Wien (Vienna),**
Wiener Fremdenverkehrsverband,
Obere Augartenstrasse 40,
A-1025 Wien.
Tel: (1) 211 144.

**Addresses of some tourist offices
outside Austria are given below:**

**Australia:**
3rd Floor, 36 Carrington Street,
Sydney, NSW 2000.
Tel: 2-299 3621.

**Canada:**
2 Bloor Street E., Suite 3330,
Toronto, Ontario M4W 1A8.
Tel: 416 967 3381

**UK:**
30 St George Street,
London W1R 0AL.
Tel: 071-629 0461

**USA:**
500, Fifth Avenue, Suite 2009–22,
New York, NY 10110.
Tel: (212) 944 6885

11601 Wilshire Blvd., Suite 2480,
Los Angeles, California 90025.
Tel: (310) 477 3332

*A mouthwatering selection of bread*

## LANGUAGE

The official language in Austria is German but the accent and some words are different. The regions are marked by strong rural accents. The Austrian diminutive is -el or -lein compared with the German -chen, so Mädchen in German becomes Mädel in Austrian.

**yes** ja
**no** nein
**please** bitte
**thank you** danke
**greetings!** Grüss Gott!
**good morning** guten Morgen
**good evening** guten Abend
**excuse me** entschuldigen
**where is?** wo ist?
**ladies** Damen
**gents** Herren
**toilet** die Toilette
**no smoking** nicht rauchen
**today** heute
**yesterday** gestern
**tomorrow** morgen
**a week** eine Woche
**a month** ein Monat
**open** geöffnet
**closed** geschlossen
**small** klein
**large** gross
**how much?** wieviel kostet es?
**dear** teuer
**cheap** billig
**too much** zu viel
**station** der Bahnhof
**airport** der Flughafen
**bus station** der Autobusbahnhof
**luggage** das Gepäck
**bank** die Bank
**post office** das Postamt
**police** die Polizei
**hospital** das Spital
**doctor** ein Arzt
**chemist's shop** die Apotheke
**danger!** Achtung!

**a room** ein Zimmer
**with/without** mit/ohne
**bath/shower** Bad/Dusche
**menu** die Speisekarte
**breakfast** Frühstück
**lunch** Mittagessen
**dinner** Abendessen
**bread** das Brot
**sugar** der Zucker
**milk** die Milch
**bill** die Rechnung
**one** (beer) einmal (Bier)
**tea** der Tee
**wine** der Wein
**white/red** weiss/rot

**Monday** Montag
**Tuesday** Dienstag
**Wednesday** Mittwoch
**Thursday** Donnerstag
**Friday** Freitag
**Saturday** Samstag
**Sunday** Sonntag

**one** eins
**two** zwei
**three** drei
**four** vier
**five** fünf
**six** sechs
**seven** sieben
**eight** acht
**nine** neun
**ten** zehn

**Glossary**
**Brunnen** fountain, well
**Dom** cathedral
**Festung** fortress
**Glockenturm** belltower
**Kapelle** chapel
**Kirche** church
**Kloster** monastery, convent
**Pestsäule** plague column
**Rathaus** town hall
**Schloss** castle, palace
**Stiege** steps, stairs
**Strand** beach
**Tor** gate, gateway

**INDEX**

# INDEX

**Acknowledgements**
The Automobile Association would like to thank the following photographers, libraries and associations for their assistance in the preparation of this book.
AUSTRIAN NATIONAL TOURIST OFFICE 21 Schönbrunn Palace, 27 Klosterneuburg, 31 Beethoven, 32 Duernstein, 34 Eusenstadt, 35 Nussberg, 38 Neusiedl am See, 41 Aggstein, 42 Zwettl, 44 Poysdorf, 50 & 53 Graz, 67 Steyr.
INTERNATIONAL PHOTOBANK 6 Faaker See, 37 Melk Abbey, 45 Ceramics, 49 Gmunden, 54 Hallstadt, 57 St Florian Monastry, 68 St Maria Wörth Church, 71 Heilingenblut, 82 Kitzbuhl, 93 Grossglockner, 119 Shrine.
MARY EVANS PICTURE LIBRARY 8 Maria Theresia, 9 Franz Joseph.
NATURE PHOTOGRAPHERS LTD 87 Little Egret (P R Sterry), 89 Great Bustard (E A Janes), 90 Alpine Chough, 94 Argiope bruennicki (P R Sterry).
WORLD PICTURES Cover Salzkammergut
All remaining pictures are held in the Association's own library (© AA Photo Library) with contributions from: P Baker, D Noble, M Siebert.